# Testimonials

So many people seek out therapy as a means to reconnect with what is truly important in life. Debbie does an incredible job in showing the reader, step-by-step, just how to do it. If you feel like you deserve a happier, more fulfilling life, *The Power Within: Claim It!* will help you get there.

Dr. David Swanson, psychologist and author of
*Help My Kid Is Driving Me Crazy:*
*The 17 Ways Kids Manipulate Their Parents*
*and What You Can Do About It*

If you feel the situations in your life are wearing you down and you see life as a problem to be solved, read this book! Debbie Miles, through this simple guidebook loaded with valuable resources, shows you how to develop your inner self, become who you would like to be, and reap the benefits! Discover your inner strengths, remove the barriers, and finally choose to live life your way.

Donna Steinhorn, life and business coach

Debbie Miles has done a splendid job providing the reader with a practical step-by-step approach to giving more meaning and purpose to one's life. She challenges the reader to embrace a series of bold and courageous changes in mind, body, and soul, and to cast off the perils of apathy, indifference, and compromise in life. This book is rich in inspiration and encouragement, and reveals Debbie's deep compassion for people. Her practical tools and strategies are vital ingredients for helping people throughout their journey to wholeness. The reader will be enriched and blessed by this special woman who is genuine in her passion to offer hope.

Hiram Keith Johnson, MA, LCSW,
author of *Tragic Redemption: Healing the Guilt and Shame*

Motivating, uplifting, and inspiring! Those are the words used to describe Debbie Miles, the work she does with others, and this wonderful book in your hands. Whether you want to find your path again or discover the brand new one awaiting you, you will definitely benefit from applying her simple strategies. The wisdom and practical advice in this book will provide *hope*, something especially needed for change. Debbie will help you see your challenges differently—as opportunities for discovery and change!

K. Alesia Willis, LMFT, LMHC

Debbie Miles has developed an excellent how-to book, filled with therapeutically sound and practical knowledge. Her work is hopeful and upbeat. Her book encourages readers who have been exposed to significant hardships in their lives to never lose hope. She provides well-designed, practical tools, which enable individuals to move forward with their lives. This work will be a welcome addition to literature in this field.

Glenn E. Rohrer, PhD, LCSW,
professor and director,
University of West Florida

Inspiring! The wisdom and practical advice in this book are uplifting and provide hope for everyone. No matter what you go through, you don't have to accept it. You can turn your challenging life situations into stepping stones to a new and wonderful journey. Apply the material, do the exercises, and you will once again own your life!

Laura Levitan, LCSW,
coauthor of BooksasBridgesInc.com

Debbie's book, *The Power Within: Claim It!*, is truly a powerful book for helping all of us not only to identify our inner strengths, but to apply them in all areas of our lives. Debbie has included simple strategies that can guide and encourage you to take action so you can live a more abundant life, and to empower you to be the driver of your life as you discover your unique strengths and talents. She challenges you to strengthen your faith and to experience spiritual growth as well. The strategies are not untested, but are ones that she has developed as her life has unfolded. She has experienced the highs and lows of life, and using these strategies has helped her maintain her equilibrium and fulfill many of the goals of her life. As a nurse, counselor, and life coach, she is well qualified to offer this book as a guide to all who are interested in improving their lives.

Chuck Randle, Pastor,
Pensacola Beach Community Church

# THE POWER WITHIN: CLAIM IT!

## SIX SIMPLE STRATEGIES TO UNLOCK YOUR INNER POTENTIAL

DEBBIE MILES

iUniverse, Inc.
Bloomington

**THE POWER WITHIN: CLAIM IT!**
**Six Simple Strategies to Unlock Your Inner Potential**



*The Power Within: Claim It! is a work of nonfiction. Client names and descriptions have been changed, however, as have identifying details of individual histories.*



*iUniverse books may be ordered through booksellers or by contacting:*

*iUniverse*
*1663 Liberty Drive*
*Bloomington, IN 47403*
*www.iuniverse.com*
*1-800-Authors (1-800-288-4677)*



*ISBN: 978-1-4759-3122-8 (sc)*
*ISBN: 978-1-4759-3124-2 (hc)*
*ISBN: 978-1-4759-3123-5 (ebk)*

*Printed in the United States of America*

*iUniverse rev. date: 11/16/2012*

# Contents

To my amazing husband, David, who gives so much of himself to others, and to my wonderful sons and their families, who make my life complete.

To my many clients who inspire me much more than they will ever know, with the hope that they too live fulfilled lives with the love and compassion from our Lord and Savior Jesus Christ, who fills us with the zest for life.

Especially in memory of my sister, Linda, who inspired so many people with her sweet smile and compassionate heart.

# Acknowledgments

The opportunity to write this book has been a blessing for me. I hope this material inspires you, the reader, to make a difference in your life and the lives of others with whom you associate. I wrote it for you and for my many coaching and counseling clients, who have taught me so much through sharing their experiences and life stories. I am thankful that my calling and profession allow me the privilege of serving people who desire to live more fulfilling and peaceful lives.

Much love to my husband, David, who encouraged me to write this book and allowed me to take over his office during this entire book-writing process. I am most appreciative of the encouragement and feedback I received from my many clients and friends. They stimulated my passion and motivated me to share this material with whoever decides to pick this book up and read it.

To Arthur Cole, my very good friend, who brought his expertise and literary magic to the project and assisted in making my dream come true. I couldn't have finished this book without his insights and support. I thank D. J. Zemenick for her expertise and patience in taking my photo for this book. She can truly work magic in her profession.

Lastly, to all of you who know that there is tremendous power within you that can guide and mold you into the wonderful person you are meant to be. Your life can be better than you ever imagined, and you can be who you want to be if you take advantage of *The Power Within*.

Often people attempt to live their lives backwards; they try to have more things, or more money, in order to do more of what they want, so they will be happier. The way it actually works is the reverse. You must first be who you really are, then do what you need to do, in order to have what you want.

Margaret Young

INTRODUCTION

# Are You Settling for Less?

> **There is no passion to be found playing small—in settling for a life that is less than the one you are capable of living.**
>
> Nelson Mandela

Do you know who you are and are you comfortable being you? Can others look at you and know you are a confident and well-adjusted person? For many of us the answer is, "No, I'm not too satisfied with who I am right now. My life could be much better."

Did you know that hundreds, even thousands, of people wake up every day and continue to give up their rights to have a successful and bountiful life? It's true. Certain people choose not to meet the challenges of everyday life because it takes too much thought, time, and energy. These are the people who are settling for mediocre lives instead of living the exceptional lives that are inside them.

Whether you realize it or not, you face a variety of mixed messages and tough expectations every day. There are 1,440 minutes in a day. Most of us have roughly nine hundred minutes (fifteen hours) every day when we are awake and alert. If you make five decisions a minute, that is easily 4,500 decisions a day! After awhile all of this decision making can wear you down and cause you to doubt yourself. That's when the caution light starts flashing, warning you of impending doom, that you are in danger of wasting your valuable life.

Let me ask you some questions. How well do you know yourself? What makes you happy? What brings contentment into your life? Years of experience as a mental-health counselor and a life coach have taught me to ask questions that force a person to dig deep from within in his search for self. If a person can't tell me who he is and what his life philosophy is, then that's my cue that this person has somehow lost his belief in himself. The inner self that directs the outer self should cause you to feel energetic, passionate, and full of inner peace, which includes the ability to reach any goal.

On the other hand, if you don't know exactly who you are and what you stand for, then how will you be able to live your life to the fullest? Will adversity and uncertainty about your decisions throw you into a whirlwind of diverse situations that end up controlling your life? After I have gathered information from my clients, all of them—men and women alike—have voiced frustration and disappointment in themselves and said that their lives seem impossible to manage. Many say, "My life is not my own!" They feel lost and alone.

Since you are glancing through this book, maybe you too feel overwhelmed and unhappy. Your life is too demanding. You don't enjoy daily tasks. You feel confused and unsure of which direction to go. You find yourself thinking, *How did I get to this point in my life?* or *What happened to the old me that could handle anything?* or *When did my life get so complicated and out of control?* or simply *I do not know who I am anymore.* If so, you are not alone!

This book is written to encourage and inspire you to take charge of your life. Today more than ever, men and women of all socioeconomic levels struggle with the feeling that they are trapped in their life circumstances at home or at work. They don't feel capable or confident enough to change things or to even entertain the idea that they have a choice. They can't see beyond their present circumstances ending up in what I call the *dungeon*—a deep, dark place where depression and other fears surface.

On the flipside, in today's society of instant gratification, no one wants to wait for change. If the results we seek don't come quickly and aren't exactly what we expect, we push aside that goal and decide to move on to something less challenging. It's easier to strive toward a goal that is simpler and less stressful. What happened to fortitude and the determination to succeed even if you have to wait? When the commitment and dedication that normally drive us to success is gone, it's easy to say "Forget that goal" and settle for less than what we deserve.

What about you? Have you reached a point in your life where you prefer someone else to make your daily decisions simply because you do not have enough faith in yourself? Maybe you feel too drained emotionally, mentally, and spiritually to deal with your life. You too might be running away from life instead of running your life!

Is your belief system holding you back? Do you believe that great success and the "good life" are meant for others, not for you? Have you given up on moving up in the world? Too many people feel they have no choice or control over what happens in their lives. When you decide to settle for less, you give away your right to envision and then reach for your dreams. I want you to know it's never too late to start over with your life. You can regain control of your life. It begins with one thought.

When I was going through my life-coach training, my mentor coach told me that everyone has the same problems, they just have different solutions. I have found that to be so true in my counseling and coaching career. It doesn't matter what nationality, socioeconomic status, or age a person is. Everyone experiences the same types of problems. These problems do affect each person differently, but the way you view your own circumstances can interfere with, or change, the way you view your life.

Each of us sees the world according to our unique perceptions. How you think and believe and how you interpret your life situations come from what you have experienced previously in your life. All of us are conditioned to see life a certain way, and it is difficult to view it any other way. You might prefer a better life, but that requires getting out of your comfort zone. That thought alone can be threatening!

This returns us to the original question I asked you: Who are you? Many people admit that they do not know *who* they are anymore. They have been too busy building a successful career or just trying to pay the bills that they somehow lost the most important part of them. They no longer live by their honorable values, morals, principles, and beliefs. Have you thrown your values by the wayside? If so, you may need to reclaim them. If you count on others to speak for you or solve your problems, you may be living your life by someone else's standards.

Being uncomfortable or unhappy with themselves or the direction of their lives is usually when people begin to do some serious soul-searching and make some changes. It might be deciding to have more time to do the things they really enjoy, living a simpler life, or having the freedom to be *who* they want to be. Everyone has the right to feel good about their lives.

You deserve the freedom to be yourself as well as the opportunity to improve the quality of your life. It is important for you to understand that when you decide to take charge of your life, you will face many challenges. You can expect difficult times ahead because change will require you to endure certain hardships. It will be worth it.

## Are you ready to change?

The decision to change or improve yourself and your life is a major lifestyle change, and it can cause others to stay away from you. It may create problems in your relationships with your spouse, family members, coworkers, etc. There is a common concept that when someone decides to transform himself, others try to discourage him because they like things the way they are. In other words, don't rock the boat!

But through the process of change, you begin to realize your new potential and develop the desire to be in charge of your life again. Some people will try to persuade you to stay just like you are. They like the misery-loves-company way of life. Why? If you change, then they might have to change. Conversely, if they do not change, you might not associate with them anymore.

You'll be reaching for higher goals and for greater awareness of yourself, while they will be left behind.

I believe that your relationships will change for the better because others will view and treat you differently. More importantly, you will see yourself differently! As your self-confidence grows, you will be better able to face challenges, and you will be in charge of your life again.

Many people want to be happy again through finding their purpose in life. Instead of just existing, they want to live a life of their choosing. They are tired of being stuck in the moment. So how do they do this? By knowing who they are and what they value. You can do this too by regaining your personal power and inner peace. You have the power within you, but maybe your fears or insecurities have taken over, leaving you weak and powerless. Together we'll find the power within you.

This book contains principles that will enhance your inner strengths, empower you to learn new skills, and provide special tools for you to use as you become the person you desire to be. Yes, you may lose some of your friends, but at the same time you will gain new friends. Hopefully, you will also experience feelings of inner peace, personal power, happiness, and the security of knowing *who* you can become.

The tools in this book are meant to encourage and inspire you to focus on your inner and outer growth. The awareness of a new and different way to think about your situations, along with new skills that bring out your inner talents, is enriching. Your outer strengths—the abilities, skills, and talents that you use as you live your everyday life—are magnified and intensified. You are more prepared physically, mentally, and spiritually to take on the challenges and risks that in the past stopped you from living a more powerful and healthy life.

Although the information in this book is probably not new to you, it is presented in a basic, straightforward way, without philosophical jargon, and with simple exercises you can apply to your life immediately. Included are examples of situations each of us face daily. You can proceed at a pace that is comfortable for you. The explanatory material feeds the mind and the Action Steps provide you with the ammunition to go out into the world and know yourself in a way you never imagined before. Seize the opportunity and take the initiative to view your life situations in a positive way and benefit from them. If you have never been in charge of your life or you somehow gave away that privilege, it is not too late to become the master designer of your new life. By taking charge again, you can create a more enriched and empowered life.

## How to use this book

People use self-improvement books differently. Some might flip to a section pertaining to their needs and start there, while others begin with the first chapter and work their way through. This book allows you to flip to the chapter that most interests you, take your time reading it, examine the examples of others who have faced some of the same issues as you, and then take time to let it soak in.

To me, this book would not be complete without adding "soul food," or spiritual insight. Within my counseling and coaching experiences, I have noticed that a large number of people (including myself) have a spiritual outlook that is a very important part of their lives. A person's spirituality includes his beliefs, needs, and a spiritual community of like-minded friends who can enhance his satisfaction and enjoyment of life.

Each chapter focuses on an inner or outer strength that we all either have or have given away. I include my insights into how and why a person might decide to give up his right to live the life that is meant for him, allowing others or circumstances to take over. I also add the experiences of ordinary people who face common challenges in every area of life—emotional, physical, and spiritual.

There are hundreds of self-improvement books full of helpful information. So many books can be overwhelming, making it difficult for a person to find the one that is specific to his needs. With my book, I recommend you take the material that you identify with best and apply it to your life situation, and then see how things begin to change for the better. Keep reading, and remember some material might not apply directly to you now but could be useful in the future. A resource section is included at the end for your benefit.

Notice the Action Steps at the end of each chapter. *Do them!* Action yields results and results lead to success. It is ideal to learn new information or reexamine facts and skills that you might have previously learned and forgotten about, but such learning is useless if you do not apply what you have learned. It is like doing homework; it reinforces what you just read. Being able to apply these steps to your life is one of the main purposes of this book.

The exercises will stimulate you to actually do the things that will move you forward in your life, change your way of thinking, and empower you in a way that you never thought possible. You can develop a new attitude and life plan that works best for your needs and wants. You will be surprised at what you can do and *who* you will become.

You and I together can identify what is holding you back from living the life that you richly deserve. Read this material to gain the knowledge and skills to view yourself in a totally different way, a way that will inspire you and others important to you. You do not have to be a genius or a millionaire to do this! The information in this book will give you the go-ahead to reclaim your confidence, or possibly gain confidence for the first time.

You can view your life differently as you discover special qualities that you possess. Don't be afraid to be a new and better person. Your strengths will continue to grow, and you will have the tools to nurture them for your benefit. Apply them immediately! These principles will enable you to live a more satisfying and fulfilling life in all areas—personal, professional, emotional, and spiritual. Feel free to share these strengths and skills with others.

We cannot predict our future or possibly know what we will have to face. I hope the following inspirational poem will provide encouragement and strength to know that you can rise above your life situations.

## Eagles in a Storm

Did you know that an eagle knows when a storm is approaching long before it breaks? The eagle will fly to some high spot and wait for the winds to come. When the storm hits, it sets its wings so that the wind will pick it up and lift it above the storm. While the storm rages below, the eagle is soaring above it.

The eagle does not escape the storm. It simply uses the storm to lift it higher. It rises on the winds that bring the storm. When the storms of life come upon us—and all of us will experience them—we can rise above them by setting our minds and our belief toward God. The storms do not have to overcome us. We can allow God's power to lift us above them.

God enables us to ride the winds of the storm that bring sickness, tragedy, failure and disappointment in our lives. We can soar above the storm. Remember, it is not the burdens of life that weigh us down; it is how we handle them.

Author Unknown[1]

Take a stand and sow your seeds of knowledge. Constantly feed and water those seeds and you will reap a bountiful harvest. Love yourself and remind yourself that you do have choices in life. You are the author of your life story. Stop settling for less and begin your new life journey!

PRINCIPLE 1

# Build a Strong Personal Foundation

*Know what you stand for and live by it.*
*Turn your challenges into opportunities.*

> **Life should not be a journey to the grave with the intention of arriving safely in a pretty and well preserved body, but rather to skid in broadside in a cloud of smoke, thoroughly used up, totally worn out, and loudly proclaiming "Wow! What a Ride!"**
>
> Hunter S. Thompson

My experience as a counselor and a life coach has helped me become more aware of the fact that people as a whole are both unique and similar to one another. We have many of the same problems, struggles, and challenges of daily living, but we handle them differently. For some of us, the roadblocks, bends in the road, and detours in life slow us down, even stop us. There are others, on the other hand, who are motivated by a challenge or hardship.

How well do you know yourself? For some, that is difficult to answer. Various clients and friends tell me that when they are going through difficult times, it is too stressful to make even one simple decision, much less attempt to manage their lives. They don't know who they are anymore. They've lost their self-worth and no longer live by their values. If this is where you are right now, don't despair. There is hope, because you can find yourself again! And as you begin your journey to know who you are and what you value, you can gain a tremendous amount of personal satisfaction.

By having a keen understanding of you, your morals, and your principles, you will develop an increased awareness of what gives your life meaning and value. These things make up your personal foundation. You may not believe it, but this foundation is where a lot of your power comes from in dealing with everyday life. It is the cornerstone of your personal and mental development. How much thought and time do you invest in this part of you?

## Examine your personal foundation

Let's compare your personal foundation to the foundation of your house. Is your house made from a sturdy material? You certainly hope so. If not, you are in for a rude awakening! If the foundation is weak, a slight pressure could cause it to crack or cave in. A weak foundation causes problems throughout the entire structure.

It is the same for a person. Do you cave in or fall to pieces when you are faced with pain or troubles? When life becomes too overwhelming or demanding, is it easier for you to turn your decision making over to someone else? If you have a weak or frail foundation that is usually what happens. When you allow others to make your decisions, you become insecure in your abilities and can even lose your self-worth. Just like a house built on a poor foundation, your life comes crashing down.

Many years ago the founding fathers of our country decided on the principles that should guide our country. They incorporated them into the Constitution of the United States. They realized that for our country to be strong and be able to withstand turmoil, its citizens needed certain values, morals, and standards to live by. Their goal was not to tell us how to live, but rather to give us the means by which to live. In the same manner, eons before our Constitution was written, another firm foundation was created. A foundation upon which, if accepted and cared for, would give everyone's life meaning and fulfillment.

Jesus realized the importance of a strong foundation when He compared someone who listened to His words and applied them to everyday life as a person who built his house on rock—that is, a strong foundation. When a catastrophe came along, that man's foundation was firm and couldn't be shaken. On the opposite end of the spectrum, Jesus warned what would happen if you failed to abide by His words. He compared this to building a house on sand. Any hardship that came along would destroy the house. In other words, we can withstand any adversity if our lives are well grounded by a strong foundation. But if there is no stability in your life, it may be because of a weak foundation.[1]

As Jesus's parable illustrates, your foundation, if firm and strong, can lead to emotional, physical, and spiritual well-being. If left unattended, a weak foundation can allow bitterness, disappointment, and pride to creep in. Which foundation will you choose?

Your life will have a much clearer meaning if you have a set of values and standards that guide you. The foundations that God, our founding fathers, and our home builders create do not force you to live in certain ways, but they all give you the means to live in certain ways. Through this, you can create your own foundation in order to build success in your life.

Your personality style will help you design your special pathway that is best suited for you. You will discover parts of you that you never knew existed! The beginning of building your personal foundation is based on your particular life philosophy. Everyone has a special outlook on life, but may not be living it. Do you know your own philosophy?

*I respect the man who knows distinctly what he wishes. The greater part of all mischief in the world arises from the fact that men do not sufficiently understand their own aims. They have undertaken to build a tower, and spend no more labor on the foundation than would be necessary to erect a hut.*

Johann Wolfgang von Goethe

## Fall for something or you'll stand for anything!

We've often heard the saying to stand for something or you'll fall for anything. The reverse seems more fitting in this day and time: fall for something or you'll stand for anything! If you do not change your way of thinking to fit with the majority of society, then you are mixed up. You are thought of as an oddball, or as someone who seeks attention or wants to create trouble.

Many people base how to live their lives on what other people think. Their values become believing that if something is popular, then it must be the right thing to do. The idea of believing strongly in their personal values and morals, their life philosophy, is no longer the norm. If you are the type of person to go along with the crowd, then your personal foundation is not built on solid ground. You have given up your right to design your own roadmap through life.

Believing in yourself and having your unique view of life will influence how you make your decisions, even if it means being different. A good example of living a one-of-a-kind life is the character Forrest Gump. If you saw the movie, you know that Forrest has his own thoughts about life. He does not think his way of life is any different from others. One particular line that Forrest says in the movie hit home with me:

> I don't know if we each have a destiny, or if we're all just floating around accidental-like on a breeze, but I, I think maybe it's both.

During the movie, Jenny, the woman Forrest loves, asks him if he ever dreams about who he's going to be. Forrest answers, "Aren't I going to be me?" His viewpoint is so simple and fits him. Think about your life philosophy. Does it fit you? Your life can be simple and easy to live. You might be wondering how, and the answer is, just by being yourself. Your passion and path are unique throughout your life.[2]

Why then does life become so complicated? What part do you have in creating your situations, or do you just have a lot of bad luck? Are you floating or drifting like a feather, landing wherever the wind blows you? Remember, as you navigate through life, you will experience different views and approaches to certain destinations or goals. You might start off "on fire" when you're young, and you inform the world to look out because you are going to make your presence known. But somehow during your journey, your spunk slowly fades away or even dies.

There are many reasons for this, and I'll discuss examples in each chapter. Your passion and your path in life are unique. They belong only to you. No one else will have the exact same path as you. Your journey will have twists and turns that will shape and mold you. It's up to you whether that is for the good or the bad!

*Any idiot can face a crisis—it's day to day living that wears you out.*

Anton Chekhov

## Life is challenging

Working as a registered nurse for many years, I was there when someone was told that her child had a birth defect, or that a husband had cancer, or that someone was facing a debilitating lifelong disease. In the 1990s, most patients stayed in the hospital for a minimum of three to four days—depending on the severity of the illness. Nurses developed rapport with the patients and it amazed me how the news affected each person differently. Some people became bitter while others became stronger. Some looked toward God for answers while others lost their faith. Their zest for life either improved or slowly died. The main question was, "Why is this happening to me?" When we are faced with a traumatic experience, we suddenly view life differently, and sometimes we never find the right answer to that question.

If you have not experienced any hardships in life, be ready, because you will. Nobody ever said life would be easy, but by having a strong foundation and faith in God, I believe you will find that you can go through anything in life and become a better person for it. It is the adversities that mold you into managing the outcomes of your life. Trying circumstances are constantly forming your foundational beliefs.

Do you recall a time in your life when something within you, an intense desire to change your life's direction, or some outside incident, became the proverbial straw that broke the camel's back? At that time you became ready to face whatever was sucking the energy out of you. You somehow found the strength to hold your head above water and get through that rough patch, experiencing blessings at the same time. It was then that you began to discover your strengths from within.

## Laura's story

Laura came to counseling because she felt depressed and lonely. She informed me that she had felt this way for years and did not know why. Her husband had been in the military and away for most of their marriage. During that time she had been the main provider and nurturer for their daughter. Her husband was now retired and her daughter had recently married. Laura believed her life changed for the worse when her daughter left home and her husband retired. She had thought since her husband was home now, they would be able to travel and tour the world. Wrong! He was ready to put down roots and be a homebody. She felt she had to put her wants and needs aside and please him. After doing that for over ten years, she felt she had no purpose in life.

Do you think Laura is the only woman who has done this? No. Have you ever neglected yourself to satisfy the needs of others? It's okay to be considerate and to help others, but not to the point that you stop living your life in order to be what someone else wants you to be. Laura stopped living by her values and principles, and instead lived the life her husband expected her to live. By the time she came to me, she no longer knew who she was or what she wanted out of life.

*Life is like a coin. You can spend it any way you wish,*
*but you only spend it once.*

Lillian Dickson

## Exercise your right

You have to realize you are lost before you can be found. Sounds crazy but it's true. It happens to you when you give up your independence to be yourself. You slowly become separated and disconnected from the life you previously enjoyed and lived to the fullest, because you chose to live someone else's dream. One day you feel good about yourself; the next day, you're miserable. You're unsure where you stand. You feel stuck. This could be the time for you to reevaluate in which direction you're going.

It does not matter how old you are or how intelligent you are. Various situations in all stages of life can limit or hinder you from moving forward. It could be in your marriage, your career, or a particular family situation. A spouse or other family member can hold you back by placing demands on you that stop you from being yourself.

As I stated previously, you may not realize you are giving away your rights until you experience certain behavior changes. You subconsciously realize that something within you is missing. The joy and satisfaction you used to find in life is gone. People have told me that they feel they only exist, that they don't have a true purpose. But everyone has a specific life purpose. We were put on this earth for a reason, and we will discuss what your life purpose means in a later chapter.

How do you lose yourself and not realize it until you're feeling miserable? This isn't uncommon, since it's usually a slow process. You are so involved in your life situation that you don't notice how it affects you. Others around you may see a change in your behavior. You don't smile as often or you don't enjoy doing things with them or anyone. Then you begin to realize you're depressed about how your life is developing. Anxiety and stress become everyday feelings that stop you from being able to make decisions and doing the things you once enjoyed. Eventually you become angry or bitter, and end up codependent on others to run your life. Losing yourself is a subtle decline, as you change from the real you to who you think others want you to be.

## Personal power—to be or not to be

This brings us back to Laura. Did she have the right to live by her unique set of values and beliefs? Did she even realize she was miserable because she was not being who she truly was? Part of the reason she felt stuck in her life, as she put it, was because she had put herself in a box and could only open the lid and peek out when she felt safe. She had changed from being independent to being dependent on her husband and others.

Laura constantly said, "I don't know *who* I am anymore!" Previously she could make decisions without hesitation and knew exactly what she wanted out of life. She could handle troublesome situations with minor stress. Now she felt weak and powerless. She only participated in activities her husband enjoyed. He did not want to do what she enjoyed, and she thought she didn't have the right to do those things either. She felt helpless. All she wanted to do was stay in bed with the covers pulled over her so no one would bother her. What kind of life is that?

*The minute you settle for less than you deserve, you get even less than you settled for.*

Maureen Dowd

By listening to people's views, I have deduced that the common everyday thoughts, situations, perceptions, or rules that have been drilled into their minds interfere with their ability to develop a solid foundation. Examples that prevent or stunt personal growth are:

- Rigid childhood beliefs about family, culture, religion
- Should of, could of
- Unmet needs, fears
- Past unpleasant experiences
- Having loose or no boundaries
- Tolerating overbearing people in your life
- Negative attitudes/negative people

These are all part of the things that make up your life philosophy and which have a huge impact on the formation of your personal foundation. But how did you acquire the values and principles by which you are currently living? Do these values truly represent your life principles or are they someone else's? The primary question for you is: Are my values significant to the way I live today?

Laura felt like she lived in a box and was only allowed to peek out occasionally. Believing her husband didn't care about her because he ignored her requests to do things that she enjoyed, she gave up the things that were meaningful to her in order to keep the peace.

In her mind, she had lost her right to state her desires or to make decisions. She felt her values and beliefs were not important. As I saw it, Laura needed to know that she did have the right to state her opinion. I told her that she had the right to live by her values, but that she had chosen to forfeit that right. She was shocked when she heard this because she always believed she had no choice. She had rationalized that if she did state her feelings, it would cause a divorce, and that was not what she wanted.

Laura's philosophy in life was to live life to the fullest, but she wasn't. The realization that she was not living by her values was a "light bulb" moment for her. She decided to tell her husband that she was going to do the things she enjoyed. She decided to travel, either alone or with a friend. Suddenly she had renewed energy. She was recharged after she realized she had choices. There was no stopping her now! She had decided to be in charge of her life again. Most importantly, she realized that she could not change her husband, but she could change herself. Laura found a new purpose for her life.

You might not realize it, but you are always gathering information about the proper way to think or do something. When you were younger, you gathered this information in the form of family values, standards, morals, and choices your parents or mentors made. Most of us take on the beliefs of our families. We put our trust in our family and believe they know what is best for us.

As you matured, your thinking patterns began to change. You realized you wanted to make your own decisions and choices.

You began to butt heads with others because you viewed things differently. By challenging others' belief systems, you decided for yourself if you believed the same way as they did and you formulated your own belief system.

As an adult you now cultivate your unique life view, which is the fundamental basis for how you live your life. I recommend that you explore your personal foundation often so you can reevaluate the direction of your life.

## Redefine yourself

*A successful person is one who can lay a firm foundation with the bricks that others throw at him.*

David Brinkley

How is it that some people face hardships and move forward without any hesitation, while others cannot seem to pick themselves up after going through a difficult situation? You could say it's in the genes or the former are simply more determined, but I have seen even the strongest of people become depressed or overwhelmed when struggling with a conflict.

Growing up with nurturing parents in a positive environment and with plenty of resources is a plus, but you can still experience success in life without these. Not having had those advantages is no excuse not to go after a fulfilling life.

A good example is Dave Pelzer. In case you do not know who he is, Pelzer's childhood qualifies as one of the worst cases of child abuse in the state of California. He overcame that childhood and is now a bestselling author. Mr. Pelzer is a prime example of how you can learn from your struggles in life, changing them into positives that make you stronger and more resilient. Frequently, I recommend his books, *A Child Called "It"* and *Help Yourself,* because these books provide lessons of hope and renewed possibilities. He developed a strong personal foundation while going through shocking adversity at the hands of the person who should have loved him the most.[3]

What are some things you can do to redefine the way your life is headed? When you recognize your life is not fulfilling, it might be time to revisit your life values and standards. Have you wandered away from them? Maybe you have adopted beliefs that are not consistent with your way of living.

W. Timothy Gallwey, in his book *The Inner Game of Stress,* coauthored with Edd Hanzelik and John Horton, shares a simple way for you to experience more stability in your life. He suggests you build a personal shield to protect you. Your shield can be made of your strongest inner strengths. For his shield he used persistence, courage, and awareness. To go along with the shield, he adds a vest of understanding and a sword of clarity. He says a person should keep his shield, vest, and sword ready at all times because life is full of adversities, arguments, misunderstandings, doubts, and fears. It is better to be prepared to handle life's situations, instead of running away and not facing them. Mr. Gallwey suggests you come up with your own unique inner strengths for your armor so you can handle any stressful situation that comes your way.

We are all born with attributes or inner strengths. God gives us everything we need to live our lives productively. You may not realize you have many inner resources because you are probably only using a few of them. We use more of these resources during early childhood. Think about how innocent young children are, how they trust everyone and see no danger in anything. And look at the imaginations they have. What happens to these traits as we get older and experience life's challenges?

Gallwey believes inner resources can be identified by using three methods. I have changed them to questions instead of statements. For something to be considered an inner resource, ask yourself:

1. Is this quality found in children?
2. Do you respect these qualities when you see them in others?
3. Do you like these qualities when you see them in yourself?

A quality found in a child would make you stronger because a child is real. Children do not know how to put on a mask yet. When you see certain traits in someone you think highly of, why wouldn't you want to emulate those traits? And lastly, how do you feel when you use these qualities? Are you uplifted and proud to be who you are?

Some inner resources are:

| Peace | Love | Compassion | Kindness | Commitment |
|---|---|---|---|---|
| Humility | Trust | Appreciation | Hope | Creativity |
| Joy | Choice | Faith | Intelligence | Imagination |

The list can go on and on. The Bible names others: loving, kindness, patience, forgiveness, trust, praise, thankfulness, sincerity, and faithfulness. Living with these qualities will surely motivate you to be the best person you can be. Your inner strengths will show through your life and will radiate to others.[4]

## Turn obstacles into opportunity

Will you be able to maintain a strong foundation when your life becomes complicated or fragile? What if you lose faith in yourself and doubt your beliefs? You might even lose the desire to make your own decisions and end up taking some wrong turns in life. How does this happen?

It does happen! Some life situation or crisis will come along and fill you with doubt or insecurity. This is what happened to Laura. She stopped living by her values and beliefs in order to be who her husband wanted her to be. By not exercising your right to be yourself, you will either give up or will have neglected to take actions to improve your life.

When you are not who you are meant to be, you slowly lose your identity. You see yourself and the world differently. Your inner strengths might ebb away. At this time, you might have to rethink what is going on in your life. Taking a different route may be necessary for you; you might need to make changes.

Hopefully, you will not lose your zest for life but will continue to strive toward a greater quality of life.

Can you change your situation? Will you be able to find yourself again? The answer to both questions is yes. First you will need to change your way of thinking to eliminate your mental barriers. Review your personal philosophy to see if you need to refine it. To change from where you are to where you want to be, you must have a clear and simple philosophy that guides your thinking, decisions, and actions.

Once your philosophy and foundation have been strengthened, you will be able to make better decisions, have a positive attitude about life, feel more confident, and take the steps that will lead you to a well-balanced life. You will know if your foundation and philosophy are right for you by your results. You will actually be in charge of your life instead of following the lead of others. The steps you take will point you in the direction you want to go. The feelings within you will be gratifying, and you will feel good about where you are headed.

If you do face obstacles that hold you back, enlist the help of your support system. Friends or family members who really care about you can be a blessing during difficult times. Bounce your feelings and ideas off them. You may be surprised to hear that they have been through some of the same situations. It is most uplifting to hear others' stories, and you will be amazed at the obstacles others have overcome. It can be inspiring.

*You never will be the person you can be if pressure, tension and discipline are taken out of your life.*

Dr. James G. Bilkey

## Perfect the present

It is not easy to bounce back after going through tough times. Whether you go through a divorce, are fired from a job, lose a close family member through death, or become disabled, you will need to accept what has happened. It can be a slow, painful process. If you stay in denial or refuse to sort out your emotions, you will not be able to move forward in your life. The healing process needs to take place.

A life crisis of any type can cause you to feel trapped or stunned, or it may inspire you to create a different kind of life for yourself. If you continually strive to develop a powerful personal foundation, you will be able to use the tools and skills from within to make major changes in your life. You will get to a point where you will see life in an entirely different way and be able to seize opportunities that you were not aware of before.

Don't give in and don't give up! Too many people believe that life dealt them a bad deck of cards and they have to suck it up and do the best they can. Too often a person becomes close minded, believing he cannot change the circumstances in his life. *Life does not have to be a problem to be solved.* It is meant to be enjoyed. You have a choice in changing the way you see yourself.

Think of a family member, friend, or celebrity you admire. What makes that person appealing to you? Is it his or her looks, brains, personality, or way of approaching life? It could be any or all of these features. Examine the good traits from this person and decide which beliefs, values, and principles are truly you or what you represent. Build on these.

What traits or values come to mind when you hear these names: Helen Keller, Abraham Lincoln, Susan Boyle, or Oprah Winfrey? All of these people are, or were, everyday people who became famous for overcoming adversity in their lives. How did they do it? They took a chance and stepped out of their comfort zones.

Helen Keller was the first deaf and blind person to graduate from college, but that's only part of it. She later became a worldwide speaker and author, advocating for others who had disabilities. Think how much more effort she had to put into daily living to do the things you and I take for granted. What a feat![5]

Abraham Lincoln had a list of adversities a mile long that he overcame before he became the sixteenth president of the United States. Among other election losses, he twice lost in elections for Congress and twice in elections for the Senate. He went bankrupt, his fiancée died, and he had a nervous breakdown.

It took him thirty years to achieve his dream of becoming the president of the United States. He had plenty of reasons to give up, but he was not a quitter![6]

Most everyone has heard of Susan Boyle, the lady from Scotland who sang on *Britain's Got Talent* and surprised everyone with her voice. She was scoffed at because of her homely looks. Her website says she has a learning disability because of not getting enough oxygen at birth. She did not let this disability stop her from appearing and singing on the show.

Ms. Boyle did not win first place, but she won first place in thousands of people's hearts. She humbled me and taught me what true courage and talent can do for someone. I think she accomplished more than she set out to do. She is successful today because she took a leap of faith and did not give up.

By knowing who you are and keeping a solid foundation, you too can overcome any adversity and be a stronger person for facing it.

Last but not least, Oprah Winfrey. It probably wasn't easy for a young African American woman to get into television broadcasting in the 1970s. Oprah came from a small town in Mississippi and went through bad times in her childhood, but she overcame that. Now look how many people she has inspired and encouraged through her show. She is a producer and a philanthropist, and she continues to share her kindness and compassion with others.

*I can't change the direction of the wind, but I can adjust my sails to always reach my destination.*

Jimmy Dean

## Finding you in the heart of life

You have the same right to change the circumstances in your life, but do you exercise that right? You might think it is okay to live a mediocre life or a life that is dictated by others, being told by others (whether it is a spouse, child, parent, or friend) what to do and how. If you allow others to make your decisions, you will end up living by their values and standards.

By having a firm values system of your own, your life will have stability. Compare a house built on rocks to being tossed around in a boat during a storm. That was how Laura felt, never knowing what was going to happen to her next. She worried how long the storm would last and just hoped to survive. When you take back your basic right to live life according to your values, morals, and beliefs, you will no longer be storm tossed. You will believe in yourself and start loving your life again. Right now, do you love your life or yourself?

Remember that life is meant to be enjoyed, which does not mean it cannot be challenging. You will reap the benefits of a healthier life by taking charge of your life. You do not need to settle for less than what you deserve!

## Regain your power

*When we are no longer able to change a situation, we are challenged to change ourselves.*

Victor Frankl

As I talked about previously, difficult or demanding situations will be a part of your life, but these life circumstances should not overwhelm you and cause you to doubt yourself. If you allow life to become overbearing, you will feel threatened and give up on your personal values and goals. It is then that your life becomes stagnant and less fulfilling. If you are a godly person, you might question your faith. You might even think, "I must be a terrible person. I did something to deserve this."

I have been told all of my life that God is not the author of confusion and adversity. He loves us, even if we are weak, confused, and struggling. He wants us to talk to Him about our troubles and give them to Him. He will guide and direct our ways. Isaiah confirms God's goodness toward us when he tells us to keep our eyes and heart focused on Him—especially during times of stress. "He gives strength to the weary and increases the power of the weak." It is important for us to keep the faith and to wait on God to restore us. Receiving comfort and renewed strength is empowering. "Those who hope in the Lord will renew their strength. They will soar on wings like eagles; they will run and not grow weary, they will walk and not be faint."[7] With this reassurance of hope and love from God, you will feel His guidance within you and be able to tackle any life situation. You will gain the strength to make it through the tough times and become a much stronger person because of what you have endured.

*One's philosophy is not best expressed in words; it is expressed in the choices one makes . . . and the choices we make are ultimately our responsibility.*

Eleanor Roosevelt

We see the world according to our individual perceptions. In other words, how we think, believe, and interpret our life situations comes from our limited belief system and how we've been conditioned to see life. If you've only been exposed to negative people and hardships, you develop the attitude that life is tough. If you received minimal inspiration or praise from your parents or teachers, you might be the type person who will not take a chance on a project because you are afraid it will be too difficult. You might think that if you fail, people will laugh at you, so it is better not to try and be safe.

Or you may have been encouraged to participate in many activities and been told that even if you did not win, it was fine so long as you gave it your best. You were admired for your accomplishments, no matter how minor they were, and grew up to believe you could accomplish anything. How you were conditioned as a child by your parents, teachers, and others has a tremendous effect on how you see yourself now.

By constantly nurturing your self-development, you can discover new and powerful ways to overcome the adversities holding you back. Ask yourself, "How can I take my life back and be *who* I truly am?"

There are steps you can take to develop your unique life philosophy. The first is to know and live your life views. This awareness makes it easier to face the tough situations in life. *The satisfaction of being comfortable in your skin enables you to be more successful in living a life of your choosing.*

Your personal foundation is the glue that holds you together. It will assist you in developing your life philosophy. As you become more secure in your beliefs, values, and morals, your foundation will become more solid. Your foundation affects your outlook on life and is expressed through your everyday actions. It's important for you to have your unique beliefs, your own way of living. People who know who they are and what they value seem to gain a tremendous energy and personal satisfaction that comes from within.

The basic principles in this book are meant to encourage you to live a more satisfying and fulfilling life. These principles should stimulate all areas of your life. If you have a life philosophy but do not totally believe it, then how is it going to benefit you? If you tell your friends that your philosophy in life is "Love life as if today is your last day," but you go around criticizing everyone and everything, they will think you do not really believe that philosophy. Your actions and your attitude are the opposite of what you are saying.

Self-belief is a must in order to live your life according to your unique viewpoint. Again, this sounds simple, but how many times do we lose faith and belief in ourselves when life feels more like a burden than a gift? We will discuss this further in the next chapter.

Whether you choose to change your specific situation is up to you. Will you be the type of person who settles for less, or will you once again pursue your dreams? You can reclaim your personal power. It's your life!

Now, take the time to do the following activities and start making the needed changes to live a life you desire. Write down your answers and begin to design and live your new life journey. Hold yourself accountable! Tell others what you are doing and ask them to assist you in whatever ways they can.

*Do not ask the Lord to guide your footsteps, if you are not willing to move your feet.*

Anonymous

## Call to Action Steps:

- Think back to who made up your first "circle of influence." Write down their names, and next to their names add whether that person was a positive or negative influence. Which people assisted in making you a better person? How? It's good to know how your core values were developed.

- Write down your most compelling beliefs, values, and morals, which you try to live by daily. Can you think of any that you have dropped by the wayside that you would like to incorporate into your life again? Write down other values and morals that you feel obligated to live by even though they are not truly yours. Decide if you want to get rid of them.

  Example: My mom believes in strict discipline, but I'm not sure I do.

- If you do not already have a personal life philosophy statement, develop one. Make it easy and simple, but make it something that describes you.

  Example: "You get what you give" or "I intend to make the best of every situation."

  - Look up positive affirmations on the Internet. You will find thousands of positive statements. Find one that fits you.

- Go to stores that sell plaques with sayings on them. Buy one that suits you and hang it on your wall at home or in your office.

- Make your own motivational board by buying a cork board, cutting out pictures or positive sayings from magazines, and tack them to your board. Update it often.

- Choose a favorite movie or song that represents how you feel about your life story at the moment and figure out why.

Example: The song "The River," by Garth Brooks, because it speaks of courage and never giving up.

❖ Design your unique personal shield with your top five inner strengths or resources. List the strengths that honor and express your values. Include each area of your life: professional, personal, spiritual, and financial. Review the part of this chapter that describes the inner resources.

Example: "My goal is to get on a spiritual path." Does this fit into your top values? If one of your values is having inner peace or being a Christian, then this goal is in line with your values.

❖ Write down your goal(s). You are more likely to reach your goal if you write it down! Design specific action steps on how and when you intend to start and finish this goal(s). Be realistic and make it fun. Celebrate after reaching each goal and this new way of life for you!

Example: My goal is to become more spiritual by September 20, 2012.

- Read my devotional book each morning (while drinking coffee).
- Pray daily before I go to sleep.
- Do one thing nice for someone daily, such as give a compliment.

Make sure your goals are simple, obtainable, and fun. If you try to change too much at one time, you may become overwhelmed and give up. Changing things in your life is a lifelong process.

PRINCIPLE 2

# Develop Your Life Philosophy

*Believe and invest in yourself.*
*Change what needs changing.*

> **If you believe you can, you probably can.**
> **If you believe you won't, you most assuredly won't.**
> **Belief is the ignition switch that gets you off the launching pad.**
>
> Life Philosophy from Denis Waitley

As I was driving to work and listening to the radio, I heard a segment that allowed children to call in and tell a joke. A young boy came on.

"Why didn't the skeleton cross the street?" the boy asked.

"I have no idea," the radio host replied.

"Because he didn't have any guts!" the boy exclaimed. The little boy laughed hysterically and said, "Get it? A skeleton is just bones. He has no guts!"

I laughed. But then, after a few minutes, I thought about how his joke could be taken both literally and figuratively. How many of us don't attempt to do certain things because we too lack "guts"? This joke can be a sober reality for some.

Life can be limited and uncertain when you have little or no faith in yourself. No one will ever know who you truly are if you never take a chance or try different things due to fear. Your self-belief is a major motivator, leading you to do the things you desire and assisting you to become all that you can be. Without it, you end up like the skeleton—without any guts!

## What's inside you?

Do you listen to your inner self? Think about how you portray yourself to others. Are you optimistic or pessimistic? Do you feel comfortable being yourself? Are you living your beliefs? It is important to monitor your way of thinking. Your mindset has everything to do with your outlook on life. Limited thinking can be the ruin of a person. You miss out on many opportunities if you choose to ignore possibilities because of negative thinking, or by listening to what others think you should or shouldn't do. What you could be or what you could accomplish will never happen if you refuse to listen to your inner thoughts and beliefs. You know yourself better than anyone!

*The happiness of your life depends upon the quality of your thoughts.*

Marcus Aurelius

You are what you think. How you think affects how you feel, which in turn determines your actions. How often do you say to yourself, "I can't do that," or "That's for other people, not me," or "I'm a failure"? These types of thoughts stop you from believing in yourself, which eventually kills your initiative to take steps toward your goals. You are a by-product of your thoughts. You can sabotage yourself by what you say to yourself. You can be your worst enemy!

The negative things you say to yourself can counter the positive things others say to you. For example, someone tells you, "Your hair is pretty," or "I think you look great in red," or "You have such a kind, gentle way with children." With low self-esteem, you will not accept the compliments because you think you are not worthy. You think the person is simply being nice and does not want to hurt your feelings. It is difficult to receive a compliment or praise when you don't believe it yourself.

Where does this negative mindset come from? A negative mindset is usually a result of self-disapproval. Why would you already have decided that you are not worthy of praise? This behavior pattern did not just start on its own. It usually begins in childhood and follows us all of our life. You decide at an early age if you like yourself or not. But how?

Young children like everyone, including themselves. Do you remember ever singing, dancing, or reciting a poem to family members because you were proud to show them what you had learned? What about when you learned to ride a bike without training wheels? I think many of us have proud memories of that accomplishment. It's one of the biggest milestones of growing up.

Most children thrive on praise; it is a form of motivation for them. Giving praise to a child is like giving water to a dry plant. Water the plant and watch it perk up! As children we see our worth through the eyes of our parents, grandparents, teachers, siblings, and others. When your parents spoke to you, was it with love and genuine interest, or was it to tell you what to do because they felt you couldn't do something on your own?

Where you fit in with your family and the world around you has a lot to do with your level of self-acceptance. If you felt appreciated and believed you contributed to your family, then you probably have a good sense of worth. Positive self-worth allows you to freely state your opinions and needs. You feel you can ask for what you want and not always be rejected. So where does negative self-worth come from?

If you spoke up as a child but were chastised for it, you might not feel comfortable today stating your wants and needs. Statements like "Who asked for your opinion?" and "Did anyone ask you to chime in?" perhaps made you think your opinion was not worth much. Eventually you developed a pattern of stuffing your desires and needs deep inside, and you felt less worthy than others. Carried forward, this pattern may stop you from giving your opinion today!

I remember when I was a young child, my mom would repeat to me, "Never think that you are better than others." She wanted me to treat everyone as I wanted to be treated, but what I sometimes heard was that other people were better than me. In order to be nice to other people, I had to put others above me and think less of myself. The result of this was that when my friends accomplished something good, I would be proud of them, but I would think that I would never be able to do something like that. I believed they had what it took, but I should not get my hopes up thinking that I did. In other words, my mother's simple statement worked in reverse. Maybe you too remember rules that were drilled into you at an early age and what affect they had on you.

I used to believe that a large percentage of the way we see ourselves came from how our parents saw us or how they treated us. I no longer believe that. I now believe that how we see ourselves is how we *believe* our parents saw us or treated us. Our perception of how we were treated could be completely different from what our parents were trying to convey to us.

## Stop the inner-*fear*-ences!

During that sensitive time of growing up, you received many messages and general directions about making your life choices. Most of that information came from your parents, extended family, church, and school teachers. As you got older, you added experiences outside of these environments. All of this knowledge and your life experiences formed the framework for your personal foundation. But what if these messages and sayings stunted your personal growth, the heart of *who* you are? I call these "inner-*fear*-ences"!

In sports when someone holds, restricts or deters the player, the official throws a flag and then calls interference. A penalty is usually involved. This interference might cause a delay in the game or a player could be thrown out of the game. These are penalties. Some of my clients tell me that they are afraid to speak their true feelings or to try something different because someone may lash out at them or they may fail. Their "inner fears" take over and they worry too much about the costs, therefore they forfeit the right to believe in themselves. These "inner-*fear*-ences" or negative inner thoughts usually win. The fear of being rejected or fear of failure is too confusing and draining.

Think back to your childhood and report-card time. If your grades were good, you probably have good memories. If your grades were not so good, well, you might prefer to forget about those times. When the grades were not acceptable, were you reprimanded with degrading questions or remarks, such as, "Are you stupid?" or "Why can't you learn anything?" or "You'll never make it to college"? If so, you probably did not think much of yourself during those times.

Those statements could have affected you in one of two ways. They might have made you question your inner worth by thinking, "They're right, I am dumb." Eventually you might have stopped trying to do your best because you did not believe in yourself. But the other view could have been, "I'll show you!" For some of us, if a parent told us we could not do a certain thing, we saw that as a challenge to prove that we could do it!

The messages that you hear in childhood stick with you forever. Unfortunately, the negative messages act like CDs being played over and over in your head. You hear these messages every time something happens that makes you feel like a failure. Conversely, every time you accomplish something, in your mind you are still not good enough.

In a football game, a referee calls interference when a player illegally hinders his opponent from catching a ball. You need to be like that referee, calling out your inner-*fear*-ences, the negative or corrupt messages that others have placed in your head.

If you continually listen to those CDs, the way you view yourself will be altered. These images will spill over into your work and other areas of your life as well. These inner-*fear*-ences will block your ability to accomplish your goals and will limit what you can become. Over a period of time they will take the zest out of life and cause you to stop believing in yourself. What you say to yourself inwardly will manifest itself outwardly through your actions or inaction.

Remember when you were a child and someone asked you what you wanted to be when you grew up? You probably didn't hesitate when you answered, because most of us were not thinking about how to get there. We were just concentrating on what we would like to be, without hesitations or limitations.

When my oldest son was four, he always noticed a young man that picked up trash from the roadsides. This young man had a stick with a sharp point on the end. He would stab the trash with the stick and put it in the trash bag he carried on his shoulder. He kept our small town highways very clean. This was his job. My son evidently thought this would be a great job, so when his teacher asked him what he wanted to be when he grew up, he immediately answered, "The person who picks up trash beside the road!" She asked him why, and he stated because he wanted a stick with a sharp point on it, so he could poke the trash and put it in the bag that goes over your shoulder. He thought it was so cool!

He eventually grew out of that fantasy, but I do remind him of it occasionally. The point is, a child doesn't concern himself with how much money he will make or what his status will be. He thinks of doing something that is fun and exciting. He has no fears or doubts.

Now, ask that same child when he is in high school the same question and he may say, "I don't know," or "I'm not too good at anything," or "I don't think I am college material." What happened to the confidence and high self-esteem that he had as a younger child? It seems like we lose our confidence and belief in ourselves as we get older. The doubts or fears (our inner fears) enter our minds and take over our healthy beliefs. This negative thinking begins to limit our choices. This is when the what-ifs start spilling over into our minds.

We defeat ourselves before we even try to accomplish anything because of the negative self-talk. Often, it is easier just to believe the criticism instead of trying to prove to others and ourselves that we are worthy. So how do we get these thoughts out of our minds, especially if we have been belittled by our family, friends, or peers for years? I admit, it is difficult to change to a new way of thinking. Years ago I read a bumper sticker: Expect nothing—it won't disappoint you! I immediately laughed, and then I wondered how many people, because of various life circumstances, actually choose to live by that philosophy.

## Today is a new day

*It's never too late to be what you might have been.*

George Eliot

Because we are living in a "disposable" era, it is easy to use something once and throw it away. We think nothing of it—disposable wipes to wash our hands, disposable diapers, cameras, razors, gloves, contacts, you name it! Wouldn't it be great if we could use a negative or self-defeating thought once and then get rid of it? Rip it out of your brain. You have used the thought, so now get rid of it! There, it's gone, out of our memory and no longer serving a purpose. Is this wishful thinking?

Dave Pelzer in his book, *Help Yourself,* believes you can get rid of the garbage in your life in the same way you get rid of your household trash. He was emotionally and physically abused as a child. But he was resilient and bounced back, becoming an author and motivational speaker, so I definitely read his words of wisdom and heed his advice. He lived through horrific abuse, but refused to let his experiences turn him into a bitter, cold person.

Mr. Pelzer compares our negative thoughts and emotional garbage to rotten food, soiled diapers, or banana peels. The negative thoughts and feelings that depress you and send your life spinning down the drain need to be thrown in the garbage can and discarded. Just as you empty your waste baskets weekly and haul your garbage to the road to be taken away, place your emotional garbage along with it. Do that over and over until it becomes a habit.[1]

Have you allowed your mental and emotional garbage to linger in your mind, rotting away your self-esteem? This extra baggage (damaging thoughts and emotions) will eventually wear you down. You'll experience confusion, you will dread making decisions, and you will end up losing your identity, wishing for someone else to take over your life. Your self-esteem and values will dwindle away. Hanging onto your emotional garbage, your harmful thoughts and behavior, is like living in a prison, where you have no privileges or free will. Worst of all, you allowed this mindless garbage to destroy the best parts of who you are.

Imagine how different your life could be if you only believed in yourself. A strong self-belief gives you the power and ability to reach your goals. You might have to study harder to pass a test, work longer hours to buy a house you really want, or go back to college after having a family, but you will be able to accomplish these things because of your determination. Looking at your situations for what they really are instead of what you perceive them to be would be a start. Nothing is impossible if you believe in yourself! You can reclaim your life by taking back the responsibility to be in charge again. It's your life, and you are the one who has to change the areas of your life that cause you unhappiness. Don't wait until a catastrophe happens.

## Change your mindset

Changing your mindset can create endless possibilities for you. Thinking of things in a different way can open doors for new and special opportunities. Do you know the definition of insanity that is attributed to Albert Einstein? Doing the same thing over and over and expecting different results! It's not what you do but how you think that interferes with your results. In my profession, I find myself repeating this phrase often because people do not realize their thinking pattern is holding them back until someone else points it out. You have the potential, although you don't think you do.

If you can't accept the fact that you will discover new and different opportunities just by changing your view of your situation, you lose your initiative to strive for a greater life. You will continue to doubt yourself and allow the inner fears to take over. Then anxiety creeps in, and it becomes too overwhelming for you to even think about entertaining new possibilities. For example, you are next in line for a promotion at work, but you turn it down, saying that you won't do well. Or someone you really like asks you out, but you make excuses not to go, thinking, "He/she is just being nice." A friend tells you about a new job and you are excited about it, but you do not make any effort to apply. Are you setting yourself up for failure?

If I tell you there is a simple way to get rid of these inner fears and that your life could drastically improve tomorrow, would you try it? Of course, you would! Remember, we are living in the age of quick fixes. On TV they tell us we can lose twenty pounds in two weeks, or that we can remove wrinkles overnight to look years younger. Do we buy these things? Yes, because we want instant results. I do not know of anyone who got the results they were promised, but I know I have tried several of the weight loss programs myself. And no, I did not lose twenty pounds in two weeks.

Let's face it, you did not become this way overnight and your mindset will not be fixed overnight. If anyone tells you that it is easy to change the way you see yourself or live your life, be wary of them. You can change the way you view yourself and live a more productive life, but it takes time and patience.

Understanding that it will take effort and commitment on your part for your life to be more satisfying and rewarding, you have to ask yourself, "Do I want to change the way I see myself and my life?" Of course, most of us would say yes . . . but not everyone. A number of people prefer to keep their lives the way they are. Why? Because it takes too much time and energy to change it!

*It's not what you go through that defines you; you can't help that. It's what you do AFTER you've gone through it that really tests who you are.*

Kwame Floyd

## Life management

Life can be a burden and be too difficult to manage. You can be changed for the better or for the worse when faced with hardships. If you ask "why me?" and fall into the pity trap, you will give up and stop attempting to reach your goals and dreams. The *why* part is not the most important, it's the *how* you plan on overcoming this problem or situation. Is the situation going to make you miserable, or are you going to fight it and become a better person for it?

I read a story on the Internet a few years ago that shows different ways you can face your life situations. The author is unknown. When I told this story to one of my clients, he named it "Grandma's Parable," which seems most appropriate.

The story begins with a teenage granddaughter telling her grandmother how difficult her life is and how she is ready to give up. After she solves one problem, others keep popping up.

The grandmother takes her granddaughter to the kitchen and fills three pots with water, placing them on burners, and turns the burners on high. When the water begins to boil, the grandmother places carrots in the first pot, eggs in the second pot, and ground coffee beans in the third pot. She lets all of them boil for twenty minutes. Then she takes everything out of the pots, putting them into separate bowls. She asks the granddaughter what she sees. Her granddaughter says, "Carrots, eggs, and ground coffee beans." The grandmother tells her to feel the carrots and the eggs and to sip the coffee. The girl does so.

The grandmother points out that the carrots are soft and weak, the eggs are hard, and the coffee has a rich taste and aroma. Each object faced adversity—the boiling water. Yet each object was affected differently. The carrot went in strong and hard but came out soft and weak. The egg was fragile, with its thin outer shell and liquid interior, but after being boiled, it became hard and solid. However, the ground coffee beans were special, because after being boiled, they changed the water. She asks the granddaughter which one represents her.

The granddaughter realizes what her grandmother is trying to tell her. You can allow adversity to make you either weak and frail or hard, or you can take the adversity and use it to your advantage. She understands that it is up to her to choose how she will react to problems. When life throws her curves, she'll decide which direction to go and whether the adversity is important enough to stop her from living her life as she chooses.[2]

Once you are confronted with hardships or roadblocks, how do they affect you? When a stressful situation or illness strikes you, do you become soft and weak like an overcooked carrot? After a death or divorce, have you become tough and hard like the boiled egg? Your outer self looks the same, but inwardly are you bitter and skeptical because of a hardened heart? Or you could be like the coffee beans and use the incident that caused you pain or hardship to motivate you to change the situation. Remember, the coffee beans actually changed the hot water by releasing their fragrance and flavor and creating a more pleasant environment.

Are you the type of person who, when things are at their worst, you see the threat as an opportunity? When your trials are their greatest, do you elevate yourself to another level? How do you handle adversity? Which one represents you: the carrot, the egg, or the coffee beans? Overcoming difficult situations and challenges makes you a stronger and healthier person. Being healthy includes developing a sound mind, body, and soul. Our minds, bodies, and souls work together to strengthen us for whatever we may face in life. No one is exempt from adversity, so we might as well be prepared. Have your personal shield ready. For my reinforcement, whenever I encounter a problem, I say, "Bring it on!" There is nothing that the Lord and I can't handle together. Refuse to allow the adversity to control you.

## Angelica's story

Angelica was a fifty-year-old woman from Puerto Rico who had lived in Florida for over twenty years. She previously worked full-time, but because she developed multiple sclerosis, when she came to me she was not able to work. She was not happy in her marriage. She received minimal emotional support from her husband and felt depressed and anxious, not knowing what would happen to her when her health worsened.

Yet Angelica was a well-educated and successful person. She had a tough time getting to where she was, overcoming many obstacles along the way. She felt she had a more difficult time than some because she was a woman from another country. Angelica previously was proud of herself and her accomplishments, but now she thought everything she had worked for was going down the drain. She had lost her self-confidence and felt worthless and trapped. She had begun to question her faith in God too.

When you face adversity, it will change the way you live your life. Your viewpoint becomes tarnished; you do not see out of the same eyes. How you see your situation will determine your outlook on life. If you view it negatively, things such as depression, anxiety, and low self-esteem creep into your mind and slowly take over your life, like any physical disease. You don't always notice as these feelings become part of your thought process.

After Angelica faced her feelings about her life situation and worked through them, she realized her future was up to her. She could remain depressed and negative, or she could do something about it. Angelica wanted to change the way she viewed herself, rid herself of her feelings of worthlessness, and she knew it would be a challenge. So how did she do it? It took a lot of reinforcing, but because of her commitment and deep desire to have a better life, Angelica developed a renewed faith in herself. After months of attending counseling, she reframed her situation from a life-threatening one to a life-enhancing one. We reevaluated her values list and added new ones. Remember the carrot? Adversity had made it weak and soft. Just like Angelica had become. But the good news was that Angelica had the inner strengths that she needed. She had simply forgotten how to call on them.

After she regained her inner strengths and abilities, Angelica began to explore her options. She decided to take chances and change the things she didn't like in her life. She wanted to be even more determined than she had been before her illness. She began to view her illness as a small part of the problem, not what defined her. Living by her principles again, she openly spoke her feelings of discontent with her husband and his lack of support, and he listened. He began marriage counseling with her. Angelica educated herself about multiple sclerosis and found out that the progression can be slow and she could live a normal life.

She eventually went back to work part-time. Committed to doing the things she enjoyed, she became a new person, seeing her life with new eyes and a different perspective. She became health conscious, adding exercise, relaxation, and fun activities to her everyday routine. She enjoyed life more now than before! She also regained her faith in God, and felt she had grown spiritually because of her illness and the things she went through in discovering her new self.

When you have feelings of worthlessness as Angelica did, it is more challenging to change the way you think. It takes a lot of reinforcing, commitment, and a deep desire to live your life to the fullest, but you *can* change. Through exploring your options and possibilities, you become empowered to face your adversity instead of giving up. It's up to you whether you choose to be strong and tough or weak and fragile.

For most spiritual people facing difficulties in their lives, a crisis or adversity does change the way they view God or their religious beliefs. Certain fears and insecurities creep in and take over. Many of us will question our faith, wondering why God has caused bad things to happen to us. We can choose to go either direction when faced with hardships: create distance from God or move closer. In some of my experiences, I first created distance, but eventually grew closer to God.

Many of my clients tell me that after tough times they usually ended up feeling stronger, and they realized that God had never turned from them. They had turned from Him. I call it the blaming God syndrome. It seems the better we get to know God, the clearer His voice becomes. His voice can be small and still and gentle, but always full of compassion. It gives us freedom. God's love for us increases our faith, which in turn allows us to plant new seeds of hope and desire. A strong desire is the fire that burns within us and enables us to do the things necessary to live a more rewarding and peaceful life.

## Tame your fears

Fear is not always a bad thing. If a wild animal comes running toward me, you'd better believe I will start running. If the brakes failed to work in my car, you would hear me yelling for miles. These situations are real and should arouse fear in us. One definition of fear is a feeling of agitation and dread caused by the presence or imminence of danger. Other definitions include feelings of distress, nervousness, anxiety or alarm caused by impending danger or pain.[3]

Did that definition imply you can experience fear from impending danger, anxiety, or feelings of distress? Yes, and you have probably felt afraid and anxious just thinking about something that could happen. Your mind can even go back to previous times in your life when you were anxious about something, and it is still so real to you that even now it prevents you from attempting tasks that you are capable of doing. Think of times when fear entered your mind and stopped you from doing something you really wanted to do. Your desire and determination left you, and you became paralyzed in your mind. You stopped thinking about facing the situation, because the fear was too real and overwhelming. Fear causes insecurity, which leads you to question yourself. You start to live your life by considering "what if." What if I try and fail? What if people laugh at me? What if they expect more of me?

*I have been through some terrible things in my life,*
*some of which actually happened.*

Mark Twain

Most of the fears within our minds we have never actually experienced. I remember one year our family vacation was to Six Flags in Atlanta, Georgia. Our oldest son was nine or ten years old and was very excited about a new roller coaster at the park. He really wanted to ride it, and he stood watching it for a long time. Our younger sons had no desire to ride it, so I told my oldest son that I would ride it with him. But he never worked up the courage to ride it.

After we returned home, I overheard him telling some of our adult friends about the theme park. He described the roller-coaster ride in detail and talked about how scary the ride had been, as if he had ridden it himself. He talked about it with so much excitement, one friend asked him, "Did you ride it?" He said, "No, but I almost did!"

That's the way we end up sometimes, almost doing something or almost facing the fear. Your inner fears are constantly testing you, and they can gain power over you. Fear steals your joy and enthusiasm.

*Put your future in good hands—your own.*

Mark Victor Hansen

## Retrain your brain

When my coaching or counseling clients are facing various life struggles, I ask them to try to look at the circumstances from a different angle. They look at me as if I've lost my mind. Then they laugh and say, "Do you mean my situation could be worse?" I say, "No, but think about how you could turn it around and see your situation from a different perspective. How can you view your misfortune differently?" By the time a person enters counseling, he feels as if he has exhausted all means of working on his unique situation.

But you can change the way you approach life. I call it Retraining Your Brain. You can redirect your way of thinking, and through this process you can face life with new enthusiasm and motivation. Take the old CDs out of your memory bank and put in a blank CD. Be ready for new, refreshing material that will inspire you to reach your dreams. It is the same concept as getting rid of the old to make room for the new.

Here is another example of teaching your brain to focus in a different direction to stimulate positive inner growth. Glen

Hopkins, owner of Motivational-Messages.com, shares his view of Tony Robbins's acronym about fear. Robbins chooses to think of FEAR as:

**F**alse
**E**vidence
**A**ppearing
**R**eal

I urge you to try it. Notice what happens each time you begin to experience fear. As doubt and anxiety enter the brain, your heart races, your palms sweat, and insecurities take over. Think of the above acronym of fear. Now, is the fear real or perceived? Mr. Hopkins believes each person should create his own definition of fear. What is your personal definition of fear? By the same token, you can also create your own definition of success and failure. What success means to others may not be success for you. Experiencing failure does not mean you are a loser. Something positive can be gained from every experience we go through.[4]

Don't allow your definitions to limit you. Try not to live by someone else's definitions either. You must be the one to control your future, your destiny. I used to hate it when people said to me that something good always comes out of something bad, because it seemed like I only heard that after an upsetting or even devastating event. Now I actually say it to others because I have found it to be true. Reframing the way you perceive things has its advantages, but it comes with a price. It will take time and effort on your part. Ask yourself these questions: How much are you willing to invest in your well-being? Are you doing it for you or for someone else? Who will receive the benefits?

You have to have a desire from within to change the way you see your stressful situations and to change the way you handle those situations. If you are tired of being on a seesaw of life, with too many ups and downs, then you are ready to experience a more satisfying and rewarding life. If you are doing it for someone else, say a spouse or a friend, it will not work.

You will want to include others in your retraining your brain process so they can help you if you start to backslide. If you decide to take on the challenge, a few of the many benefits you will gradually receive are:

- Boost your motivation in life
- Personal growth in all areas of your life
- Develop the courage to live your life according to your values
- Be honest in expressing your true feelings
- Cultivate a path that will allow you to be your best self

Try to see every challenge as an opportunity for change. If a certain situation is not benefitting you, then examine it and see if you need it in your life. The same goes for things that have happened in the past. If you have memories of unpleasant experiences and they bring you down, leave them in the past. You are what you make of yourself. Remember you're in charge, and don't let other people or circumstances determine your destiny. Change starts with you!

*Nothing limits achievement like small thinking; nothing expands possibilities like unleashed imagination.*

William Arthur Ward

## Start with what you know

Can you imagine what your life could be like if you explored the new opportunities that are available to you? Look around and see what resources are available. Resources do not have to be tangible things like money or friends. You can start with a simple belief in yourself. We have talked about how having a firm foundation and personal philosophy will guide you in making better decisions. These are powerful inner strengths.

Simple, small steps make a big difference in the way you face your battles. For example, using positive phrases such as "I can,"

"I will," or "I am" is powerful. When you wake up in the morning, say aloud, "I can be successful. I will be successful." When fear and doubt begin to creep in, continually say these positive statements to yourself, and say them out loud! It's said that you need to do something for twenty-one days in order to develop a habit. Make this day one. Make this the day your self-esteem is elevated. It does not take much energy, and it becomes easier and easier the more you practice. The more positively you think, the easier it is for you to reach your goals.

*Power is the ability not to have to please.*

Elizabeth Janeway

## Unlock your power

It's important for each of us to realize and say, "I am ultimately responsible for the quality of my life." This is probably not a light-bulb moment for any of us when things are going well. It's when things aren't going so well—such as a job loss, problems with children, financial issues, or an illness—that we choose to blame others instead of accepting our part in creating these situations. Putting the blame on others for the dilemmas we face is common. Just watch the nightly news. You'll hear case after case of crazy, out-of-control, lawsuit-happy people! No one wants to take responsibility for their actions anymore. We easily rationalize that life is unfair and the blame belongs to others, not us.

It's difficult to see anything positive in your life when you feel powerless. You don't want to face your responsibilities; that's too draining. When you feel vulnerable, it may help to think about 2 Timothy 1:7—"For God hath not given us the spirit of fear; but of power, and of love, and of a sound mind." This is a reminder that if we hang in there, we will regain our power, our love, and our minds. Yet when things are too hectic in our lives, these spiritual gifts seem to disappear.

This next paragraph, written by Marianne Williamson, expresses her feelings about how you can handle your fear, whatever it is.

> Our deepest fear is not that we are inadequate. Our deepest fear is that we are powerful beyond measure. It is our light, not our darkness, that most frightens us. We ask ourselves, Who am I to be brilliant, gorgeous, talented, fabulous? Actually, who are you not to be? You are a child of God. Your playing small doesn't serve the world. There's nothing enlightened about shrinking so that other people won't feel insecure around you. We are all meant to shine, as children do. We were born to make manifest the glory of God that is within us. It's not just in some of us; it's in everyone. And as we let our own light shine, we subconsciously give other people permission to do the same. As we're liberated from our own fear, our presence automatically liberates others.[5]

If only we could stamp parts of that speech in the palms of our hands and read it daily! When you are highly confident in yourself, it's easy to believe that you can conquer the world. Nothing can stop you. Not to say that you won't have struggles and face roadblocks. You may have to change your course from time to time, but you will continue to strive to reach your goals. Lose that confidence and see how life will begin to weigh you down. As we have discussed, how you envision and choose to handle your everyday challenges will play a huge part in whether you let go of and boost your inner strengths.

As Williamson says, "let your light shine." Others will take notice and it will rub off on them. When you keep forging ahead even while facing hardships or difficulties, others take notice and become empowered because of your strength, your refusal to give up. You are an example and inspiration as you live your life, and you might not even realize others are using you as their model of how they want to be one day. There's nothing more impressive or inspiring than when someone who is oppressed and downtrodden turns his adversities into strengths, finding ways to overcome and prevail. The ability to be resilient unleashes your power within, and a crisis becomes a motivator instead of a roadblock.

## Understand your emotions and invest in yourself

Understanding our emotions and what they are telling us in whatever situation we are in is an important factor in reaching our greatest potential. In her book *What's Really Holding You Back?*, Valorie Burton discusses the importance of unlocking the messages behind your emotions (anxiety, depression, insecurity, pride, anger, etc.). If you're afraid someone will make fun of you or humiliate you if you speak up about your likes or dislikes, you tend to agree with others and keep your true emotions inside. You prefer for others to tell you what to feel. Giving up your right to proclaim your feelings puts you on the path to losing yourself. It is a self-defeating process, and if allowed to continue, you will not even know who you are anymore.

Many of my clients sabotage themselves by demeaning themselves. They don't believe they have anything of significance to offer, so they minimize their strengths and refuse to accept that they are valuable and respectable people. I have heard the phrase "God doesn't make junk" for most of my life. I do not know who is credited with that statement, but I believe it. He created us in His image, and the Bible tells us that He loves everything that He created. God values each of us in our own special way, and if we could see the value in ourselves as well, we could look at the world through totally different eyes.

*Take time to gather up the past so that you will be able to draw from your experience and invest them in the future.*

Jim Rohn

Your life experiences are molding you into *who* you can be. Do you "push the envelope," or are you content to remain in your comfort zone? Why do I ask? Whether you realize it or not, you grow from the defeats you might suffer by extending yourself and pushing the envelope. Conversely, if you always stay in your comfort zone, you become jaded and stunted, even if you always win. Sounds ridiculous, but it's true! Think about it this way: When you accomplish everything you attempt, maybe you are not aiming high enough. If you always stay in your comfort zone and never reach out for goals beyond those limits, your growing stops. In other words, you're not making any investments in your potential.

Let's take a closer look at this. Can you remember times when you gave it your all, but still lost? Tried your best to get a certain position at work and it didn't happen? Studied for a test that you needed to pass, yet failed by only a single point? Did that feeling of defeat cause you to want to try harder the next time? If you answered yes, as I hope you did, that's investing in your future. By being spurred on by failure, not giving up or giving in, you continue to push yourself to exceed your goals and have the belief in yourself that you can achieve whatever you put your mind to. You may not succeed—this time—but there's always another chance.

Remember this: What benefit is it to have an inspiring life philosophy built on a solid foundation, but have so little faith in yourself that you won't put it to work? Self-belief is a tremendous motivator that allows you to put your values to work. A solid foundation not only makes you who you are, but assists you in becoming what you can be. So take daily action to incorporate your self-worth and effort into your daily life. Digest the information in this book to start you on your way.

Follow the Action Steps and use them to design your new life. Eat, sleep, and breathe them until you create a new and unique life system. I've presented another list of Action Steps at the end of this chapter to get you rolling, but feel free to add your own to them. After all, it's your life, invest in it! Again, hold yourself accountable and take advantage of the new things you learn about yourself.

## Call to Action Steps:

- Be familiar with what's inside you. Evaluate the situations or problems you are facing and decide if you want or need them in your life. Are you able to use these situations to your advantage, or do you need to come up with solutions to eliminate them for now? As you focus on what you want and don't want, make sure you are including your values. If not, get rid of the things that are taking the place of your values. Continue to add to your values. Here are more examples of values:

| | | | | |
|---|---|---|---|---|
| Health | Forgiving | Courage | Playful | Self-Disciplined |
| Organized | Neat, Clean | Orderly | Optimistic | Solitude |

There are many others. Think of the way you are—or of the abilities you have—that come naturally to you. Add to your list often.

- Become more aware of your thought processes. Pay attention to what is happening in your life that causes you to think negatively. Write down your negative thoughts. On another column, write a statement that turns the negative thought into a positive one. Practice doing what it takes to make the thought positive. Hold yourself accountable by telling your friends and family members that you are working on changing your thought pattern. Ask them to point out every time they hear you make a negative comment.

  Examples of negative or limiting thinking:

  - You see changes at work as problems: "We have a new boss and things will never be the same."
  - If you don't succeed at something, you think, "Forget it, it's just not meant for me."

- Constantly thinking, "I can't make these changes" before you even attempt to do something differently.

❖ Now that you are aware of your negative thoughts, what can you do to stop this way of thinking? Remember the Retrain Your Brain material? It's time to reframe your situation and actually take the steps to get the results you want. Ask yourself these three questions when your thoughts prevent you from moving forward:

1) How much am I willing to invest in my well-being?

2) Am I doing it for me or for others?

3) What benefits will I receive?

Next, write down the benefits you desire. Remember, the results and benefits are up to you. The more you invest in yourself, the better your life will be. Be aware of who you are becoming and enjoy working on your new self.

❖ Recognize the fears that are holding you back. Write down your goals and dreams and decide if your goals are worth facing the fear. Maybe the fear is not as frightening as it seems. Write down the costs (sacrifices) plus the benefits (success) of reaching your goal and decide if the fear (whatever it is) will hold you back. Is the pain worth the gain? If you can't get rid of the fear, maybe now is not the right time to work on this certain goal. Move to another goal and come back to the one that is causing you distress.

❖ Take time to watch motivational movies of people who overcame obstacles in their life to become *who* they wanted to be. Take note of how they developed strengths to face their fears. There are hundreds of inspiring books you can read as well.

Examples:

*The Pursuit of Happyness*, *The Miracle Worker*, *To Kill a Mockingbird*, *The Bucket List*, and *Norma Rae*. Look up other motivational movies on the Internet.

- The greatest book ever written tells us to "Ask and it will be given to you; seek and you will find; knock and the door will be opened to you."[6] How strong is your faith? What are some ways you can strengthen it? Your faith will lead you to pray for guidance in your everyday thoughts and actions. Pray daily and thank God for your blessings. Keep a journal of your prayers and write down your blessings from the prayers. You may be surprised when you see how blessed you are.

- Find people in the Bible who inspire you and ask why they seem special? What did he or she do? What did he or she do when faced with adversity? What valuable lesson can you learn from the way this person lived his or her life and apply it to your life?

  Example: Saul was a cruel man early in his life as he went around persecuting Christians. Later, he was struck blind by God. He immediately asked God what He wanted him to do. God told him to stop persecuting his people! Saul, his sight returned, immediately turned from his wicked ways to follow Jesus. He became a wonderful apostle and example for others. Saul, who later became Paul, proved you don't have to be a perfect person to be a disciple of Jesus. Like Paul, I want to live my life as an example of how you can have faults and still be an inspiration to others. You too can keep the faith and always strive to help others.

PRINCIPLE 3

# Recognize What's Holding You Back

*Take the initiative to face your fears.*
*Find your motivation for success.*

> **You have brains in your head.**
> **You have feet in your shoes.**
> **You can steer yourself any direction you choose.**
> **You're on your own. And you know what you know. And YOU are the guy who'll decide where to go.**
>
> *Oh, the Places You'll Go!* Dr. Seuss

## Stop the whining!

When my clients sit on the fence because they're not able to make a decision—because they feel guilty or insecure or for any other reason—I tell them a story about how being miserable is a choice. Read on:

> There was an old man who sat on his front porch in a rocking chair every afternoon with his miserable old dog lying beside him. He sat there for hours. One of his neighbors noticed that as the old man sat there, his dog whined continuously, but the old man did nothing

> about it. The neighbor finally went over to the old man and said, "Neighbor, I notice that every day your dog whines and you do nothing about it. Why is he whining?" The old man told him it was because the dog was lying on a nail. The neighbor, stunned, asked him why the dog didn't move. The old man said, "I guess it don't hurt badly enough!"

Are you hurting badly enough to do something about it? Or would you rather sit on the fence, leaning one way for a while and then leaning the other way, but never making a decision so you can get off the fence? You continue to feel nervous, unsteady, and miserable because you don't feel the situation is bad enough yet. Most of us are content to be miserable, until something drastic comes along and pushes us out of our comfort zone.

The most common excuses people use to justify not making decisions are: "I just don't feel motivated," "If I could get excited about facing my challenge, I would work diligently to change things," or "It's just not the right time." Yes, it is much easier to make excuses about why you can't do this or that, instead of just doing it. Do your excuses remind you of the whining dog?

I have whined like that dog on the porch. One of my friends was going back to nursing school to become a registered nurse and she wanted me to go with her. She and I were already licensed practical nurses, and we would get paid much better if we went back to college. She hounded me constantly because she was ready and she wanted me to go with her. I had three small sons at the time and I did not want to leave them with a sitter. Eventually the children were in kindergarten and elementary school, and therefore I no longer had the same excuse not to go to college. I was nervous about going back to school, as it had been ten years or more since I'd been in college. But for every excuse I came up with, there was a solution. I finally realized it was time to go back. It took me two years, but I got my degree.

The rewards are well worth the time and energy you put into reaching your goals. It's great to have a strong personal foundation and unique philosophy, but if you don't have the initiative (guts) to take the steps to reach your goals, you'll never know what could have been. You'll automatically expect less from yourself and settle for less. If you refuse to act on your ideas and notions because you doubt your ability, then you might as well plan on being miserable, like the dog lying on the nail. You must realize that your time is limited, so don't waste it living a life that is mediocre. Stop whining and make the decision to change the things that are holding you back and preventing you from enjoying life.

*A mediocre idea that generates enthusiasm will go further than a great idea that inspires no one.*

Mary Kay Ash

## Take the initiative

Steve Jobs, cofounder of Apple Inc., is a great example of someone who had an idea and ran with it. He wanted everyone to be able to have a computer in their home, so he decided to develop affordable computers. Mr. Jobs was only in his twenties when he began Apple Computers with Steve Wozniak and Ronald Wayne. According to an article in *Time* magazine in 1996, Jobs said, "The thing that drives me and my colleagues is that you see something very compelling to you, and you don't quite know how to get it, but you know, sometimes intuitively, it's within your grasp. And it's worth putting in years of your life to make it come into existence." The rest is history![1]

Steve Jobs believed in himself, ventured out, and took a big risk. He had the initiative to do something about his compelling desire to change the world. I've heard many stories of how someone suddenly got an idea (while driving, in a dream, or in the shower), actually carried it out, and thereby became a different person. Their lives were changed for the better. You may be thinking this kind of success only happens to celebrities or millionaires. Not true! Success can come to you if you dig deep into your inner and outer resourcefulness to create a new life and a new you.

## What's within you?

One of the things we ignore the most is our natural abilities. Your instincts will come to life if you are optimistic, positive, and have a sense of curiosity. Being inquisitive is wonderful. Children ask a lot of questions because they want to understand and learn new things. What happens to that adventurous part when you become an adult? Have you lost interest in exploring exciting possibilities, or are you fearful of admitting you just don't know? If that's the case, you need to ask yourself why.

Exploring and learning adds variety and excitement to life. To look at challenges in a different light changes the way you view your circumstances, most times for the better. If you lose your enthusiasm and desire to grow, you may repeatedly close doors on opportunities that come but once.

But if you choose to move forward facing life's challenges squarely, you become more aware of talents within you that you wouldn't have otherwise known you have. The key is initiative. You can't be afraid to open new doors. You know in your heart what you are capable of doing. It's not lack of ability or potential that prevents you from moving forward and enjoying a more fulfilling life. It's simply the lack of initiative.

## Approach life with enthusiasm

Margaret Renkl, freelance writer and editor, believes that curiosity is a natural impulse that displays itself in two ways. First, it gives you the urge to experience the fresh feeling of newness; second, it helps you regain the feeling of originality within your life. In other words, it allows you to experience life through a whole new set of eyes and ears. Every day can be a new adventure.[2]

People who want more out of life are more inquisitive. They ask more questions, seek out answers, and are not afraid to have "inquiring minds"! Being inquisitive or curious can spark a new desire within you that encourages you to search for something new and different in life. By cultivating your curiosity, you awaken your natural abilities that feed your mind, body, and soul. The need to experience newness in your life challenges you to take creative steps for a better future. Try to do things that bring out your adventurous side. Don't be afraid of what others will think. Feed your need to be courageous and step out of your comfort zone, or you miss out on some wonderful opportunities. Being curious allows you to:

1. change the way you face your challenges and new awareness to come alive;
2. build a fire within you that ignites your desire to work on any situation;
3. develop better coping skills;
4. reap the benefits of a better future.

But what if you have already lost your enthusiasm about certain things in your life? Maybe you were enthusiastic at one time, but someone or something took that away from you. Now you feel more comfortable just accepting whatever life throws your way. What kind of life is that?

If there are certain situations that cause you to be less enthusiastic about life, this negative pattern of behavior might have started in your childhood. Were you controlled by others or emotionally knocked down every time you tried to better yourself? Did you continually feel rejected or belittled? Have these childhood experiences made you give up and allow others to make your decisions? If that's the case, you have come to rely on others for almost everything that affects your life and behavior. You have surrendered your life to them.

But then again, if you take life too seriously, it can be easy for you to ignore your positive daily experiences or blessings. Therefore, make time to enjoy the simple things in life. Life goes by fast enough because of the stressors and responsibilities we think we have to tackle daily. As you are working on improving yourself or your life, do not underestimate the value of being content. There will be times when you should take time off, rest, and forget about your responsibilities for a while. Sometimes I have to remind myself that God created the entire world in six days and then decided to rest on the seventh day! God saw everything he had made and liked it, so you too need to be proud of your accomplishments and reap their benefits. As they say, “Stop and smell the roses!”

No doubt you will still encounter tough times that cause you to doubt your decisions or change your attitude from positive to negative. But these times will not last. Your growth and satisfaction with yourself will outshine the doubt and uncertainty. A statement that many of my clients live by is, “This too shall pass.” That’s a good way to look at it. Nothing stays the same. If you are not constantly changing and growing, your life becomes stagnant and boring. Remember, it does not matter what adversity you have faced previously in your life. You can begin where you are, with what you know, to become who and what you want to be. Never give in, give up, or give away your right to live your life your way.

## Regain your fame

To become a healthier person mentally, physically, and spiritually, start practicing optimism. Regain your enthusiasm; take back the reins to your life. Create and set your own goals and find the initiative to reach them. Use your core skills to overcome obstacles that you thought were insurmountable. Begin to see life’s challenges as opportunities. You have the choice to accept things the way they are or to change them.

Challenge yourself by accepting whatever situation is thrown your way. Face your problems, but remember that you do not have to do it all by yourself. Ask God to help you. Remember He tells us to ask Him for help and it will be given to us; to seek and we will find; to knock and the door will be opened. If you don’t ask Him for help, you deny yourself the guidance and love of the greatest counselor, peacemaker, compassionate comforter, and healer of everything in your life. Having peace and an understanding of who you are and what you can be are extra benefits, thrown in at no cost. With God as your personal advisor and leader, you can't go wrong.[3]

It is as important for your spiritual well-being to be fed and nourished, as it is that you take care of your physical, emotional, and mental health. If you rely only on yourself, eventually you may lose your desire to improve your life. It may mean that you have to take whatever comes your way, instead of designing the path that you desire for your future. By settling for less and wondering if you have a purpose in life, time is wasted. You end up drifting along, wondering if something good or bad is going to come your way, instead of taking charge and creating possibilities and new paths.

Remember that being curious allows you to see things differently and gives you the spirit to explore new avenues and learn new ways to do things. If you feel stuck or forget how to be adventurous, think back to a time when you faced a difficult situation. How did you work through it? What did you have at that time that you do not have now? What's different now? The most frequent answer is "no motivation." If motivation is lost, it's difficult to think of anything working out for you. It takes too much energy to think positively, much less take action.

## What drives you?

When you feel stuck or have no incentive to improve your life, think of this story. A football player—either a professional or an amateur—gets up early every morning to work out. He runs and lifts weights so he will be strong and ready to play football when the season begins. He trains four to five hours a day. It doesn't matter if it is one hundred degrees or below freezing, he continues to train.

What motivates him to do that? Do you think he wakes up every morning all excited and saying to himself, "Oh boy, I can't wait to go work out"? I don't think so! If he's a pro, some people would say his motivation is money. If he's an amateur, some people might say he wants to make it to the pros and be famous. But if you asked that player what his motivation was for working out and training so many hours a day, he would simply answer, "Results."

The athlete has a deep inner feeling of accomplishment when he makes a great tackle or stops the other team from scoring. He feels good when his team wins because he had a part in it. He is happy about being in great physical shape. His greatest satisfaction comes from within, and that is what drives him when he plays football. He truly enjoys the game and does not mind putting forth the extra effort to reach his goal. That's why he gets up early every day and works out. His wants, needs, and desires are important and motivate him, just as yours should for you.

Motivation usually occurs when there is a powerful desire to change something in your life. This powerful desire is the driving force that brings to the forefront the problems or situations that are stopping you from facing your challenges. Realizing that change needs to occur is a giant step, but if you lack the initiative to take some action steps to reach your goals or create change, it won't happen. Together, we'll not let that occur.

## Stay in the race

My middle son was the type who did not have to study much and still made all As. His goal was to go to college, get a job that paid well, and hire a maid to clean his house! He received a four-year scholarship to any college in Florida, as well as a scholarship to a local junior college. What an accomplishment, and we were so proud of him.

However, he decided after one year of junior college that it was more important for him to have a new truck and a full-time job. He informed us that he was sick of school. My heart was torn apart; I could not believe he was giving his college education away. He had worked diligently through his high school years to earn those scholarships. I talked with him daily, pleading with him not to quit. It was to no avail. He quit and found a job. He liked the job and bought himself a new truck. My dream of him being a college graduate was shattered! He lost his initiative and his motivation to obtain a college degree.

Eleven years later, the economy was taking a turn for the worse and he was experiencing cutbacks in his job, which meant a lower, or even no paycheck. He realized he had no choice but to keep his job and take whatever was thrown his way because he had very little college education. That situation prompted him to want to better himself. He finally took the initiative to go back to college, no matter what he would have to give up until he finished.

As I said previously, the driving force behind motivation is that powerful desire to change something in your life. My son's fear of being without a job, of not being able to provide for his family, and of having to take whatever was available caused his motivation to increase tenfold. He decided to go back to college. He took the initiative to talk with a guidance counselor to see what he needed to do to get his degree. He didn't know how he could do it, but his desire to get out of his current situation kept him motivated.

After you take the first step, the rest of it gets easier. Once you change your mindset, believe in yourself, and then do something about it, your motivation will return. My son continues to take classes, studies diligently, and is making all As again. The moral of the story is to never give up because it's never too late! He will finish in a few years and have the satisfaction of working a job he loves and feeling more confident about himself and his abilities.

According to authors Germaine Porché and Jed Niederer, other things motivate us besides a powerful desire to change something in our lives. These authors emphasize five major factors that they feel will boost your motivation.

1. **Recognition**—we all like to be acknowledged when we achieve something. We like to be appreciated. Self-improvement is enhanced.

2. **Challenge**—facing up to whatever we need to do. Confront and tackle the obstacles that are preventing you

from moving forward. For example, make better grades, change your career, find a better relationship, etc.

3. **Self-Development/Knowledge**—uses every experience as a stepping stone for growth and to broaden your knowledge base. Experience increases knowledge. Self-esteem is boosted.

4. **Reward**—envision the benefits and results you will obtain from achieving your goals in life. The benefits will far outnumber the risks.

5. **Fear**—face the fear. Use fear as a motivator instead of an inhibitor. Recognize and do something to free yourself from the specific fear that is keeping you from achieving your goals.[4]

Remember that something positive is gained from most, if not all, of our life experiences. Fear can be used in a positive way to produce positive energy, which in turn can produce positive results. However, if fear becomes too overwhelming, it can halt your progress. When you do something to minimize that fear and make it manageable, then you can work through it. Sometimes this is easier said than done!

*Action is a great restorer and builder of confidence. Inaction is not only the result, but the cause, of fear. Perhaps the action you take will be successful; perhaps different action or adjustments will have to follow. But any action is better than no action at all.*

Norman Vincent Peale

## Face your fear

Say you are offered a job that you really want. The problem is it includes public speaking and you have a fear of speaking in public. You love the other aspects of the job, so what to do? Is the job important enough for you to take the initiative to face your fear, or will you let this job pass you by? Take action. Talk with your friends, brainstorm, and come up with some solutions. One solution could be to join Toastmasters. This organization is great at helping people develop communication skills, which in turn foster personal growth and confidence.

What I want to help you do is to be able to recognize a specific fear that blocks your personal or professional growth. Fear often restricts a person's ability to make a decision. You may be lingering in a situation because you are afraid of making a mistake; afraid that your decision may hurt someone else and you do not want to be responsible for their unhappiness. Or you might fear that you will be rejected by others because of your decision. These inner-fear-ences slowly creep into your consciousness.

You may think it is better to leave things as they are, easier to give in and accept things as they are. You try to convince yourself that things aren't that bad, even though you are miserable. Now your growth is stunted because of your fear of the unknown and your doubts about your abilities to make good decisions. You've lost your motivation. You've surrendered to fear just as you surrendered to those who wanted to control you. It's the same thing.

What about consequences? Worrying about consequences provokes more fear! For example, you might be in a relationship in which your partner constantly threatens to leave you or to kick you out if you do not cater to his or her wants and needs. These threats create fear. You become paralyzed and do nothing to change the relationship. You feel you have to do whatever the other person says, perhaps because you are afraid of being alone or you are financially dependent on him or her. For whatever reason, fear stops you from being able to consider other options. You feel stuck!

## Jason's story

When I met Jason, he was thirty years old and suffering from anxiety because he felt stuck in his life situation. He had a good paying job that he liked, but he was required to work the afternoon shift. He didn't like working evenings because he had a six-year-old daughter, and his job prevented him from spending time with her. He lived with his fiancée—in her house—with her two sons. She took care of his daughter when he was at work. When Jason was told he was next in line to get on the day shift, he was excited. His fiancée was not so happy about it because he would make less money. She wanted a larger house.

They argued often about money. His fiancée threatened to end the relationship if he took the day shift. When he tried to discuss his feelings and ideas with her, she refused to listen and told him to find somewhere else to live. His mind was filled with doubts and fears. Should they get married? Would it be best to forget about buying a house? Fears of the unknown and of making the wrong decisions were preventing him from moving forward with anything in his life.

Jason didn't want them to set a specific date to get married because he thought they needed to work on their relationship. He was also afraid to push the house issue because he was concerned his fiancée might get upset and call off everything. He wanted to work the day shift, but what would his fiancée do if he switched. What would be best for his daughter? Who would take care of her if he left his fiancée? Everything was swirling out of control!

When he came to me, Jason was ready to confront the fears that were making him question his future. He was tired of not being in charge of his life, of constantly worrying about doing or saying the wrong thing. He truly loved his fiancée, but didn't share her views about their future. What if she really did leave him?

After Jason began counseling, he could share his feelings with me objectively, without fear of retaliation. Slowly he figured out that he was putting himself in a situation that caused unbearable pressure.

I asked him to think about what the worst thing that could happen if he and his fiancée split up. His main fear was that he didn't know who would help take care of his daughter when he was at work. This fear was so stressful, he couldn't think of other options. We brainstormed; he came up with several ideas. He had forgotten some friends had previously offered to keep his daughter if he needed assistance. Or he could move closer to his parents. He began to feel better after he worked through his fears. His motivation to change things within his control helped him to view his life in a different way. He felt more positive about expressing his feelings to his fiancée; and if the relationship dissolved because of that, he believed it would be okay.

Jason and his fiancée talked about his feelings, his fears and his concerns about their relationship. She was able to voice her own concerns, and they both felt it was better to call off the engagement for now. Jason was able to get a transfer with his company and live closer to his mother. His mother welcomed the opportunity to have time with her granddaughter and with Jason. He felt more secure with himself and was happy he had faced his fears. Jason used his fear as a motivator to improve his life.

Now, think about a time when you were going through major changes or challenges. Were you ready to face the consequences of making those changes? Maybe you had a devastating health condition. Or someone in your family was facing a life crisis. You might have needed to end a relationship or your job required you to relocate. If any of those things happened today, would you be able to face your fears or would you be ruled by your fears? Fear definitely plants negative thoughts in our minds. Your confidence in your abilities diminishes. Fear will control you if you give it the power. If you allow the what-ifs to rule your decisions, you will back down from any creative idea or opportunity. You may end up missing out on wonderful gifts that are meant for you. How can you put the fear in its place so you can go about feeling comfortable living your life?

*Let others lead small lives, but not you. Let others argue over small things, but not you. Let others cry over small hurts, but not you. Let others leave their future in someone else's hands, but not you.*

Jim Rohn

## Take charge of your mind

First, you need to acknowledge the fearful thoughts in your mind because they are real. You do not need to understand why you are afraid, just that you are. Feel free to open up and talk about your feelings with others. Having fear is not a character flaw; it is simply a defense mechanism. If you keep the fear to yourself, it will only worsen. Don't keep it a secret!

Now that you are aware of the fear, the next step is to *stop* thinking about it. What? I know I just said to think about the fear and now I'm saying stop thinking about it. I have a good reason for telling you to do this. It is part of a cycle. Recognize the fear, stop the fear, and then prepare yourself to be in charge of the fearful thoughts. How? Let's see.

Theresa, another counselor and a friend, taught me this tool, and I use it often with my clients. I use it for myself as well, and it works. Hold your index finger up in front of your face and imagine it as a red stop sign. Whatever fearful or anxiety-provoking thought you are thinking at that moment, *stop* it and replace it with a pleasant thought. Think of an enjoyable experience or visualize a scene that helps you to relax. Examples: a peaceful beach where you watch the waves wash in and out, or standing on a mountaintop looking out at the beautiful scenery. Some people like to use their sense of smell and imagine they smell freshly baked chocolate-chip cookies. Hey, use whatever works.

Now that your mind is thinking something pleasant, ask yourself these three questions:

1. Is the fearful thought reasonable?
2. Is the fearful thought rational?

3. Is the fearful thought logical?

Most of the time the answers are no! After answering these questions, you will realize that you are not being reasonable. Your fears are taking over your awareness. When you fear a new adventure or task, change your mindset instantly to thoughts of courage, strong will, and self-control. Do these steps consistently, and before you know it you will have developed a new habit. You will have a fresh outlook on how to deal with threatening or unpleasant situations in your personal or professional life. Entertain positive thoughts of reaching your goals by doing the things that intimidate you the most. Challenge yourself to go the extra mile and aim higher than expected. Begin to see your life in a new way.

Remember to use this simple three-step formula when fear is your motivator:

1. Recognize the fear;
2. Identify the fear;
3. Confront the fear.

## If you don't use it, you lose it!

Parables illustrate real life in such simple, understandable ways. There is a parable in the book of Matthew that illustrates the importance of using our talents. A master goes on a journey and leaves his three servants in charge of his property. He tells them he will be gone for a while, but he will return. To the first servant he gives five talents, the second servant receives two talents, and he gives the third servant only one talent. According to the master, each received talents according to his ability.

In this story, "talents" are a unit of money. But while the parable is about money, it illustrates much more.

When the master returns, he asks his servants for an accounting. The first servant doubled his five talents to add to the original five talents; the master was very pleased. The second servant gained two more talents to go with the original talents, and he also received praise. However, the third servant informed the master that he had been afraid, so he had buried his one talent. He dug it up and gave it back to the master.

I like this story because it illustrates what we are talking about. The moral is to use your talents, whether you have many or few. Instead of using his talent, the third servant let his fear take over. He took no action except to keep the talent safe, which to him meant burying it. He was afraid to take a risk. Maybe he had a fear of losing, fear of being hurt by the master, or fear of being embarrassed. I might have felt the same way. When your fears control your outcomes in life, life becomes unmanageable.[5]

## A cure for fear

Don Colbert, MD, in his book *Deadly Emotions*, discusses how fear and anxiety affect our brains and our bodies. He relates how fear causes stress, and being overly stressed makes us vulnerable to many health problems. Included in these health issues are: high blood pressure, diabetes, heart disease, stroke, and cancer. I don't know about you, but if I have a choice, I would not pick any of these diseases or problems.

Dr. Colbert believes faith is the overall cure for fear. His definition of faith is to continually believe that God is in charge of all things, and that if we can put our trust in Him, He will do what is eternally best for each of us. Most of us have our own definition of faith. My pastor once said he believed faith is the result of our experience and our relationship with God. I can identify with that definition because when I feel close to God, my faith is greater and my life seems to be happier and more fulfilling. Conversely, when I have ventured away from God, my life seems more difficult and out of control. I realize then that I need to get back on the right course.

Jesus says that if we have faith the size of a mustard seed (very small), we can move mountains and that nothing is impossible for us. It would benefit us to reevaluate our faith system often, especially before a crucial time comes along and rips our faith apart. A deep faith allows you to be stronger, assists you in thinking more positively, and reminds you to let go and let God take care of you.[6]

Don't be afraid to take risks. The fears you face can be enough of a motivating force to push you out of your rut. Not taking any action is worse than taking action and making a mistake. We learn from our mistakes.

*The highways of life are filled with flat squirrels that couldn't make decisions.*

John Maxwell

You have the choice to stay where you are or to advance to the level you desire. It is up to you. Life can be compared to a game. If you focus more on the results you desire, like our football player did, rather than fearing the amount of effort that you need to put into the game, you'll become more motivated in achieving your specific goals. So don't dwell too much on the amount of energy and time you need to devote to reaching your goals. Instead, think only of the rewards and results!

As you continue to strengthen your personal foundation and live by your unique life philosophy, you will have a greater initiative to be in charge of your life. Know your strengths, both the inner ones—self-confidence, courage, etc.—and the outer ones—skills, talents, etc. Trust them and take advantage of them daily. Follow your gut feelings, and when you feel the powerful desire to improve or change things for the better, take charge! A greater self-awareness guides you to your special purpose and mission in life.

Can you envision how you want your life to be? Are you focused on reaching your goals, or does fear and insecurity overrule your desires? The following Action Steps can be your guide in moving you forward or in rekindling your enthusiasm to take charge of your life. Focus on the importance of your life mission and how you can enhance it. Let's continue to build your strengths through these Action Steps. Work on them at your pace and stay committed.

## Call to Action Steps:

- Think about projects or goals you have been putting off because you lack the initiative. Make a list of your top three goals and then write down the pros and cons of reaching them. After you reach your top goals, write down your next set of goals.

| **Pros or Advantages of Reaching My Goal (Rewards)** | **Cons or Disadvantages of Reaching My Goal (Costs)** |
|---|---|
| | |
| | |
| | |
| | |
| | |
| | |
| | |
| | |
| | |

- What motivates you? Review the list of motivators and see which ones work for you. Make a list of things that inspire you to take initiative. What results would you like? Write down things you have been putting off because of a lack of initiative. Tackle them one by one. Work at a pace that is comfortable for you and remember to reward yourself after you accomplish each one.

  Examples: A better life, more freedom, more choices in life, more money, less stress, less clutter, a better job or relationships, etc.

- Become a “born again” optimist! Learn to appreciate and enjoy life to the max. Look on the Internet or in gift shops for motivational sayings. Make a list of empowering thoughts and put them in a place where you can view them easily. Write up a positive saying that represents you and tape it to the dashboard of your car, your bathroom mirror, your computer at work. Look at it often. Live by it!

- ❖ Make a list of your fears—real or imagined. Focus on how these fears make you feel and what part the fear is playing in your life.

  Example: You don't speak up at work because you are afraid you may get scolded in front of coworkers, or even fired. Brainstorm ways in which you can focus on this fear differently. Include your spouse or friends. Come up with suggestions that would lessen your fear.

  Perhaps your spouse can play the role of your boss. Practice how the boss would react to different suggestions or situations. Make it fun. Make it a way to learn your strengths and weaknesses. Ask yourself what the risks and benefits of facing your fear are. What is the worst thing that could happen? What is the best thing that could happen?

- ❖ If you are spiritual, there are many encouraging Bible verses, such as, "Be strong and courageous. Do not be afraid or terrified because of them, for the Lord your God goes with you; He will never leave you nor forsake you."[7] These are such comforting words to remember, especially when facing stressful and difficult times. How wonderful to know that you are special and that you are not alone in your times of doubt and fear. Fear has been an issue since the beginning of time, and the words "fear not" are used many times in the Bible. Look up verses that are significant to you, memorize them, and use them to help you get over your fears. Keep them in places where you can look at them often.

PRINCIPLE 4

# Pursue Your Purpose and Passion to Create Your Unique Life Path

*Identify and cultivate your inner strengths and life gifts to uncover the real you.*

> **We all have to start with ourselves. It is time to walk the talk. Take the journey of making very difficult decisions. Start removing things from your life that are not filling your cup and adding things that bring joy in to your life.**
>
> Lisa Hammon

## Life is a journey

Do you enjoy taking vacations? Some people do, others don't. I like to take adventurous road trips, although I am not too good with a map. I blame it on my fifth-grade teacher because she failed to properly teach me directions. Somebody has to take the blame! So when I get directions from someone, I like it if they tell me to turn at the McDonald's or look for a certain billboard. I don't do well with east, west, north, or south. According to other women I have discussed this with, I'm not alone here.

Thanks to modern technology, we no longer need to use maps. We have GPS (global positioning system). I have one, but

I get lost using it too! Nothing is 100 percent perfect, although these systems do seem better than a map. Isn't it a shame that we don't have any internal GPS that would always know where we are in life? Let's see what we can do to make one.

## The path we are traveling

While searching on the Internet for sayings about life paths, I found a website called the Art of Everyday Wonder. The words on this site express the importance of having your unique path in life instead of following others. These words stimulated and evoked a variety of feelings within me, and I wanted to share them. See what feelings they stir up within you.

> But looking too hard for the one, true path can create its own problems. You can find yourself fixed on finding "the" answer rather than noticing and enjoying where you are. The search can stop you from noticing the path that is unfolding under your feet. It can get in the way of you recognising, and honouring, the trail you have left behind. And it can leave you focused on external pointers and signs, rather than trusting your instincts and intuition to find your way. Joanna Paterson[1]

Don't forget to be as passionate about the journey as you are in reaching the destination. Have a vision for where you want your path to lead you. Envision it, dream it, and then begin your trip. Feel free to be led by your unique desires. Don't be afraid to go around curves and expect detours. Prepare to reap bountiful results and don't let anyone get in your way. Life is short, so get started!

## Be ready for roadblocks

Life is one long journey that can take you wherever you want to go. How you live your life is up to you. It is not an easy concept for some people to grasp. You may see life as adventurous and enjoyable, but if you are miserable and consider life a constant burden, you probably feel you have little or no control over what happens to you. In fact, you have more control than you know in living your life. Your choices, your decisions, and your attitude predict which direction you will take. Generally, do things run smoothly for you, or do you feel you have to fight for everything you get? Why are some people successful with every venture they attempt while others have to jump through hoops to get any benefits?

If you are living your life purpose, your life will fall in place no matter what situation you are facing. You will truly enjoy your life. Many of my clients say they do not know if they are living their life purpose. They feel bored or lost, and are not passionate about much in their lives. Living seems to “suck the life” out of them! Most of them are facing a major roadblock in their life journey. It’s up to them to choose whether to stay where they are or change their path. It’s the same for you too.

Some people prefer to believe that no matter how much extra effort they put into life, it is not going to change for the better. They think they can do nothing about whatever comes their way. Forget about reaching your dreams, they say. Accept the fact that your destiny is to struggle and to endure a difficult life. Is that you?

Let me tell you, it is easy to fall into that trap. My life journey was going along just fine until September 16, 2004. The previous weekend my family had celebrated Labor Day and had a large family birthday party. Little did we know it would be the last birthday party at that house.

If you live in sunny Florida, you become familiar with hurricanes. In my area, Pensacola, we are most familiar with hurricane season, which begins June 1 and ends November 30. Every year we have warnings and watches, but usually we get lucky as the storms head off in another direction. That time we were not spared. Hurricane Ivan hit, and for days we were subjected to heavy flooding, forceful winds, and strong follow-on storms. It was the fifth costliest hurricane in United States history. There was major damage to homes, schools, and businesses. Roads were closed and there was no electricity for weeks. The

National Guard was called in because of the vast destruction. People died and many, many homes and businesses were ruined. Almost everyone's life was changed.

Our home was destroyed. The roof blew off and the house flooded. Because we lived near the beach, we were not allowed to go see what was left until two weeks later. The roads had been so damaged by water and high winds, you couldn't even tell where they were. Downed power lines were everywhere. The devastated beach and city would need to be rebuilt.

Out of all the devastation, what hurt me the most was that I'd forgotten about the thousands of family pictures stored in boxes under a bed and on shelves in a downstairs bedroom. After surveying our damaged home, I thought about the pictures. When I recovered them, all of them were soaked. They had already been sitting in water for two weeks! I cannot describe how distraught I felt. Would life ever be the same?

*We make a living by what we get, but we make a life by what we give.*

Winston Churchill

## Your life gifts

You probably have your own stories of devastating things that have happened to you. Right now, you could be facing a detour or roadblock, or looking for a new route because of a serious health issue, a bad decision, or a divorce. With the foundering economy, you might be faced with losing your job or home. Think of times in the past when your journey was interrupted by someone or something that you had no control over. Did it cause you to completely change your life direction?

When you had that experience, were you truly enjoying your life before your journey was interrupted? How successful were you? Did you feel you were doing your best at whatever you did, or could it be that you weren't working toward your mission in life? Were you headed down a one-way street in the wrong direction? Did someone else have a greater plan for you? Wow, so many questions!

I ask these questions because the answers will help you know if you are using your unique gifts as you go about living your life every day. The answers might help you understand your mission and purpose in life. Your life trip may take you in directions you never thought of or even considered. Detours, as the highway people call them.

Now, I don't know about you, but I don't like detours. I like the familiar way. I like to stay in my comfort zone. With detours you go into unfamiliar territory and start worrying about making a wrong turn. Yet some detours in life provide a better route. They offer changes that will benefit you, instead of slowing down your growth and development. Sometimes people or obstacles are put in your path to urge you to rethink your priorities—to take a detour. Is it a blessing or annoyance? The choice is yours.

In *The Five People You Meet in Heaven*, Mitch Albom tells how certain people, family members or strangers, can change our path in life. His main character, Eddie, felt bored and trapped in his life. His job was meaningless, and he felt lonely and miserable. Eddie was put in the path of a young girl for the purpose of saving her life. He lost his own life to save her. He didn't know who she was and she didn't know him. This book reminds us how our lives affect others, whether we realize it or not.

When your life becomes too stagnant, watch out! That is probably when some incident will occur, changing your life in ways you could never imagine. We like order and structure, the ordinary and familiar situations and people of everyday life. For you to experience life to the fullest, you have to push yourself and extend your potential. That is when you'll discover what your special gifts and talents are. And when you use your life gifts combined with your special ministry or calling, your life will have greater meaning and impact not only for you, but others you meet along the way. It causes a ripple effect.

Each of us is born and designed with a specific purpose. We have been given spiritual gifts to help us live fulfilling lives. In the Bible, we are encouraged "to live a life worthy of the calling you have received."[2] The Bible talks about different kinds of gifts, services, and works. Most importantly, everyone receives a gift for the purpose of being uplifted. Some of the gifts mentioned are wisdom, knowledge, faith, and prophecy.

In his book *What You Do Best in the Body of Christ*, Bruce Bugbee has a long list of spiritual gifts. Some of them are administration, creative communication, encouragement, discernment, knowledge, music, leadership, teaching, and wisdom. Mr. Bugbee explains how using your gift enables you to excel not only in your personal life, but in your professional and spiritual lives as well. If you are not using your gifts, you will not be doing the things meant especially for you. This could explain why some people do not enjoy their lives. Think about your day and how you spend your time. I mentioned previously we have 1,440 minutes in a day. How you use them is up to you.[3]

In her book *Jesus Life Coach,* Laurie Beth Jones reminds us that Jesus wants us to be fruitful, which in this day we translate to mean productive. Notice that I said "productive," not busy. It seems we live in a time in which busyness is the norm, but does being busy always mean being productive? You can be one of the busiest people in the universe, but how much do you actually accomplish? Ms. Jones illustrates this difference —accomplishment vs. productivity—by using the example of a fruit tree. When a tree bears fruit, it is being productive. Unlike the fruit tree, when you accomplish something, you put forth effort in achieving or obtaining whatever it is you want to attain. So to produce results, you actually exert your energy and time.[4]

A fruit tree generates its fruit naturally. The fruit is in the tree; bearing that fruit is the tree's main purpose. We could say it is a process instinctual to the tree. Now think about what you do instinctively. How productive or creative are you? How much time do you waste doing things that are not important or doing things that do not add value to your life? Are your tasks done in an effortless way like the fruit tree's, or do you have to work endlessly to accomplish your goals?

Let's return to those life gifts and see how they might relate to the fruit tree. Does your life flow smoothly as you do your daily tasks at work and at home? If so, you are probably using your natural spiritual gifts or talents. What you do at work, home, or in church will seem effortless when you use your gifts. Life seems to fall in place easily for you.

One way to know whether someone is using his spiritual gifts is by the way he answers general questions about his life. Ask someone why he goes to work every day, and he might say, "I need a paycheck" or "I have bills to pay." These answers indicate the person is not doing a job he loves. But when someone answers, "My work brings out the best in me" or "I love what I do so much, I would do it for free," you are talking to someone who truly enjoys his job. He is using his gifts through his profession and doing what he was designed to do. You will have a special feeling of satisfaction when you are providing a meaningful service that you are passionate about.

I believed I was using my spiritual gifts in my work and personal life, but I wanted to verify it, so I took a free spiritual assessment on the Internet. The assessment asks you questions about yourself, instantly records and analyzes your answers, and then you get your results. My assessment was so me! I e-mailed it to family and friends, and they could not believe how close it came to who I am and to what I do daily. There are many spiritual assessments on the Internet. My favorite is at www.churchgrowth.org. It is not difficult to take, it's free, and you get your results instantly. Share it with others who know you and see if they agree with the assessment. Most importantly, see if you are using your gifts. How do you know if you're using them? Most of the time, if you are enjoying your work and your life, you are!

Many books are written about spirituality and using your spiritual gifts. Two that I recommend are *What You Do Best in the Body of Christ* by Bruce Bugbee and *Spiritual Gifts: Their Purpose & Power* by Bryan Carraway. Remember, spiritual talents are qualities that you possess, not activities you perform. These talents are within you, you already use them daily, and you probably do not recognize them as gifts or talents.

## Turn problems into potential

Every day you make decisions. These decisions constantly mold you into the person you are. Your choices and your experiences are unique to you. Your past experiences have a lot to do with how you view situations today. How you respond to a situation is also partly learned behavior. How you choose to view your past and present experiences determines which road you will take. Your perception of life is usually formed through how you see yourself and your unique situations.

If you have had negative experiences and have become bitter, you will not feel comfortable taking chances. It is easier for you to keep things as they are and live a mediocre life, instead of trying to improve your life. You worry that you might fail and that others will think less of you. Your spouse may be intimidating and discourages you from becoming your best self. You may be stuck in a certain situation and think there is no way to do any better, so you give up. But let's see what can happen if you don't give up.

## The donkey in the well story

I enjoy telling people how I learned an important lesson from a donkey. It gets their attention. This story is called "The Donkey in the Well." Since I could not locate the author to give him the credit, I will tell it in my own words.

One day a farmer's donkey fell into a well, and the farmer did not know how to get the frightened animal out. The farmer was frantic. The well was mighty deep, and he just could not think of a reasonable solution. Finally, he calmed himself and began to do some thinking. The donkey was old and the well should be filled in to prevent this from happening again. He gave up on the idea of rescuing the donkey and believed he should simply fill in the well. The farmer did not want the poor animal to suffer, so he persuaded himself that this was the right thing to do.

He quickly told his neighbors about the incident. They grabbed their shovels and along with the farmer began shoveling dirt into the well to help cover up the donkey. When the donkey realized what was happening, he moaned and kicked, but after a while, he got quiet. Everyone believed the donkey was covered in dirt. The farmer decided to look down into the well, and was shocked when he saw the donkey was still alive. Actually, the donkey was close to the top of the well! The donkey had noticed that each time he shook the dirt off; he could step on top of it and be nearer to the top. Soon the donkey was able to step up over the edge of the well, and he happily trotted off.

The poor farmer had thought he was doing the donkey a service by eliminating his suffering, but the entire time the donkey was turning it into a way to get out. The moral of the story is that when life seems impossible, do not give up. The trick is to shake it off and move on![5]

If a donkey can turn something potentially deadly into a positive experience, then I think I can do it too. Do you give up too easily and let life's situations win? Are you too exhausted or not confident enough to stand firm and fight the fight? Giving up is the easy thing to do, but it could cost you immensely. What would have happened to the donkey if he had given up?

Your life is shaped by your many experiences, and most of your experiences are the results of your decisions. But how does the way you make life decisions relate to the donkey? How can you turn adversity into advantage? Problems into potential? Here I go repeating myself, but I want you to get the point!

## Confidence or emotions?

Most of your decisions are driven by two things: your confidence in your ability to achieve a certain result or goal, or by your emotions. As a rule, emotions usually guide your decisions and override your self-confidence.

A common example: you want to lose fifteen pounds and you feel confident you can do it. You have a diet plan, so you know what foods you can have and what times you can eat. You do pretty well for two weeks, but then one day you are stressed over something that happened at work and you begin to eat things that are not on your new diet. This situation upsets you even more, and you continue to eat the wrong foods because of the emotional stress. What happened to your confidence? What won, confidence or emotion? As in this example, most of the time emotions override confidence. So to truly enhance your life, it is beneficial to work not only on the abilities and skills that build your confidence, but that also build an awareness of your emotional reactions.

Some people hold a misconception about self-confidence. They think being self-confident means you have to be able to do anything and handle everything. To do that would take a superwoman or superman! This thought pattern is why some people do not attempt certain challenges that could have a positive impact on their future. In fact, being self-confident really means you know you may make mistakes, but also that you will learn from your mistakes.

The most common emotion that affects how you overcome a roadblock or face a challenge is fear. Fear of making a wrong decision should not prevent you from moving forward in your life. If you allow fear in, you end up thinking of yourself as a failure instead of someone who faced a challenge and learned from it. Confident people will face a challenge. Fearful people won't. Confident people learn and apply what they have learned. Fearful people can't.

Through careful monitoring of your reactions to situations, you can find it easier to be in charge of your life situations. You become more aware of your emotions—good and bad. Be aware of what makes you want to dive into a problem or steer away from it. The ability to understand the emotions that control your thinking can give you the ability to deal with them.

## Frank's story

Frank, a forty-six-year-old Canadian, complained of being in an irritable mood most of the time. His girlfriend constantly told him that he was moody and carried his feelings on his shoulders. Frank said he didn't like tolerating employees who did not follow through on what he instructed them to do. I told Frank that sounded reasonable. I would not like it either.

Frank owned his own contractor business, and he expected his employees to understand everything he said the first time and just do it. He did not like to explain anything to anyone twice. He considered people irresponsible if they did not understand his orders. He also didn't care to hear their personal problems when they informed him that they would be late or needed to take a day off. Frank told his employees if they weren't happy with the job, they could leave.

In other words, he was very impatient and demanding of others. He felt others should fear him because, in his eyes, fear meant respect. He did not consider his employees' feelings when he demanded things from them. Imagine how many employees Frank has gone through over the years. Would you like to work for Frank? Not me!

I told Frank he was a demanding and cold boss. He said he had been told that before, and even his girlfriend said he treated her the same way. He was one of those people who believed "my way or the highway!" He came to me because he realized his behavior was causing problems in his personal and professional life.

I understood Frank's disgust when he felt people weren't listening to him and having to act as a parent instead of a boss. But how inappropriate was it to treat people the way he did? He made it clear to his employees that he did not care about their personal lives and did not have any empathy for them. Most of his decisions were based on his emotions—what mood he was in—not his self-confidence. He understood that he caused most of his problems by not having any self-control.

At least Frank knew his behavior pattern was causing problems for him. Self-awareness allows a person to see that he needs to make changes in his life or he will continue to be miserable. He came to counseling seeking guidance to improve his behavior because he wanted to improve his relationships at work and at home. He was tired of being frustrated and wretched most of the time.

After several months of counseling, Frank learned how not to be self-centered, and realized he needed to care about the feelings and needs of others around him. He began to ask his employees their opinions and listened to their suggestions. His employees felt valued. This took some of the pressure off Frank, and he was relieved that his employees were now more responsible and loyal to him. He learned the importance of having faith and trust in others.

Frank began to identify the thoughts and feelings that caused his negative emotions. He decided to live by his positive values and beliefs, and wanted these to be the driving force of his emotions. By doing that, he could communicate better and feel more connected with his employees and with his girlfriend. He realized he had a choice in how to react to situations, and that his choices would determine how his day would be. Eventually his life was more enjoyable. This process began because Frank made a decision to change.

Remember, the direction of your life is determined by your decisions. Evaluate your decision-making techniques, analyzing whether it's with your emotions, your self-confidence, or a mixture of both. Don't be afraid to reach higher or go the extra mile so you can happily manage your destiny. Learn from the donkey. Take the obstacles in life and turn them into opportunities. Your next decision may be a life-saving one!

## Growth is a process

Stephen Covey, internationally respected leadership authority and author, believes that as each of us lives our lives, we look through our own "unique lens of experience."[6] We interpret our lives as we have been conditioned to see things. When someone disagrees with us, we automatically think something is wrong with them. We think our perception is the right one and we try our best to win others over to our way of thinking. Changing your perception is tough!

You see this often with parents in raising their children. Each parent tries to instill his and her unique beliefs and opinions in the child because that is what they believe is right. When the child becomes a teenager and wants to develop his own way of doing things, the parents often reject those ideas. Why? Because they were conditioned by their own experiences and those of their parents. Some refuse to reexamine their beliefs, listen to others, or be open to others' ideas—especially their children's.

Think back to times when your beliefs were challenged. We learned in school that people at one time thought the world was flat. Wow, imagine what went through their minds when they found out the world was round! What about when people speculated that a man would one day walk on the moon. It was amazing to see that first person on the moon. This event changed the perception of not only the people of this country, but of the entire world! These events prove we are what we are conditioned to believe.

What you think, say, and do is specific to you. Do any two people think exactly alike? What would life be like if everyone acted the same way? I remember when I was a teenager and was asked, "If so and so jumped off a bridge, would you do it too?" You are probably familiar with this question. It is a universal reminder for us not to follow others and to think for ourselves. Personal growth comes from being able to make your decisions based on your values, morals, and beliefs. Be true to yourself. Be a leader, not a follower!

*We aren't just thrown on this earth like dice tossed across a table. We are lovingly placed here for a purpose.*

Charles Swindoll

## Know your purpose

Your life experiences may have a direct connection with your special gifts in creating your life purpose. God created each one of us with a unique plan. No one else's life will be the same as yours. Everyone is created with the same body parts (heart, brain, eyes, etc.), but how you use these parts is specific to you.

How you see things and interpret your life experiences is based partly on how you saw your parents and other family members live their lives. But it's also how you are made on the inside. The saying "It's what's on the inside that counts" is very true. How you see the world on the outside begins with *who* you are on the inside.

I love planting flowers and then watching them as they grow and bloom. Sadly, not every plant lives. Some die a few days after being planted. To me, it's the luck of the draw. Bruce Bugbee says when plants do not flourish, it is easy to assume the problem was with the plant. The gardener watered and fertilized it but it still didn't grow, so something must have been wrong with the plant. It's easier just to place blame on the plant instead of focusing on other reasons why it didn't do well.

Could something else be wrong? Do all plants grow because you simply stick them in dirt and provide fertilizer and water? Wishful thinking, but no! I have wasted valuable time, effort, and money on planting plants that then wither away and die. But if a plant is planted in the right environment, it will survive and produce as it was created to do. Sounds easy enough, but how do you know if you are planting it in the right environment? Educate yourself by reading about and studying the plants before you buy them. How simple that is, although I did not think to do that for years. If the plant was pretty and smelled sweet, I wanted it in my yard. Now I have several books about plants, and I read about them before I go to the gardening store.

Mr. Bugbee takes the point a step further by illustrating how people need the same components for proper growth to occur. Is your work or home environment favorable for growth? Are you living or working in an environment that limits or prohibits your knowledge? Or one that does not provide you with the proper tools and resources for you to be fully who you are? If so, your personal and professional growth will be stunted. More than likely, you will lose your initiative and your inner desire to be fruitful, and you'll feel incomplete in your life. You'll probably feel frustrated, less confident, and confused about what to do. Ask yourself these two questions: Do I know what I need for proper growth? Do I put myself in the right environment?

## Maria's story

Maria, a thirty-year-old woman from Ecuador, was miserable with her life. A few years earlier, when she still lived in Ecuador, she married a man from Florida. They decided to move from Ecuador to Florida right away. Maria willingly quit her job as a store manager, left her family behind, and learned to speak fluent English, excited about exploring new opportunities that she did not have in Ecuador.

Her husband worked offshore and was gone for a month at a time. Since Maria did not have many friends at first and felt lonely, she decided to look for a job. She searched for months and could not find a job she felt qualified to do, so with encouragement from her husband, she decided to go back to college to study nursing. After a few weeks of school, she began to have panic attacks. She felt intensely uncomfortable going to classes and being around people she did not know. She was shy and did not make friends easily. She became withdrawn, anxious, and depressed. Maria dropped out of the nursing program.

When she came to counseling, she said she felt "weak" for the first time in her life. Back home in Ecuador, she had her family, friends, and church members. Now she was all alone. Her behavior was out of control, and she felt like a failure. While her husband was away at work, she frequently felt afraid and worried about being alone in her home. Maria believed she had lost her purpose in life.

Maria was right. She needed to rediscover herself, because she was in a different situation and environment. While she was making all those changes in her life, her passion in life had changed also. When someone like Maria lacks self-confidence and self-esteem, day-to-day challenges appear too demanding. The things she had first seen as opportunities had turned into roadblocks.

The good news is that Maria did go back to college, which was one of her goals when she came to Florida. This time she took business management classes, and that motivated her in finding a job that used her skills. She enjoyed working in retail stores and decided to find a job in that area. She eventually landed her dream job. Her life felt more manageable as she found her life path and life purpose. Maria no longer felt lonely and useless.

As Maria was finding herself, she faced her roadblocks —moving to a different country, learning a new language, and leaving her support system behind—and she didn't give up. She used her inner strengths of courage, stamina, and determination to keep her focused on her goals. Her desire to regain her self-worth and the need to live through her life purpose kept her charged up to live her life's dream.

Maria's life philosophy was to never give up, even if life was one big problem after another. She already possessed the inner strengths that she needed to succeed, although it was difficult for her to recognize her talents when going through her setbacks. She just needed guidance and encouragement at times.

What about you? Will you forge ahead to reach your life goals by jumping the hurdles, or will you by stopped by life's barriers?

## Enhance your life

If you are living your purpose in life, you will be a better person in all areas of your life. Your performance at work will be better, your marriage will be enriched, your spiritual strength will be intensified, and your self-confidence will be enhanced. Even your relationships with your friends and neighbors will be more satisfying. You will know because you will feel good about the way your life is going. Things will flow smoothly and you will be passionate about what you are accomplishing. It fits you!

However, if you are not enjoying your life and feel miserable in your profession or in your relationships, you may not be living according to your life purpose. Are you happy with the direction your life is headed? If not, it may be time to rethink your priorities and ask yourself, "Exactly what do I want in life?" Do you have dreams and visions of your future, but deep down you feel these dreams are impossible to reach? Your daily activities at home, at work, and at play should bring out your natural talents and strengths, which then guide you toward being enthusiastic about life. Have you lost your enthusiasm to discover new and better ways to make your life more fulfilled? Maybe you've decided to settle for less. You put in just enough effort to whet your appetite—but no more!

*What lies behind us and what lies before us are tiny matters compared to what lies within us.*

Ralph Waldo Emerson

## What is your passion?

Your inner strengths compose a major portion of what and who you can be, as well as what you can achieve. You may want to review the chapter that discussed inner strengths, but keep in mind that living in a healthy environment and being committed or passionate about life are equally as important. Each of us is given a certain passion, calling, or meaningful purpose in life.

To me, passion is a desire that God places in each of us and that energizes us. Our passion pushes us to make a difference in a particular area of our life or ministry. Finding your passion can be a process. Not everyone knows instantly the things that bring out the best in them. When you are living your purpose, you feel contentment, happiness, enthusiasm, and intense energy, because you are living life through your passion. Not only will you benefit daily by having a fruitful life, but your friends, coworkers, and family members will benefit and be enriched because of your talents. Most importantly, you will glorify God through using your special strengths and gifts.

Think of some causes you have supported in the past. Maybe you attended meetings or campaigned for things you strongly believed in. If you have children, you probably advocated for causes that will improve their schools. This passion comes from within and once you identify it, it does not go away.

Naturally, not everyone is passionate about the same things. You may be passionate about political issues while others are passionate about the homeless or abused children. Should you be passionate about everything? I do not think you can be. You can care about and donate money to many causes, but being passionate means committing yourself to a cause. It is what you as an individual care about the most.

If you try to be passionate about everything, you could end up confused, overwhelmed, and drained. That is what happens when you try to be all things to all people! Some of my clients tell me they do not know what their passion is. I ask one simple question: What do you spend most of your time and energy on? Whatever they answer, they light up when they talk about it. They say they never complain about how much time they donate to this cause. I have found that in almost all cases, everyone is passionate about something, and they show it by meeting the needs of a certain group of people, animals, or things.

I read a story in a newspaper of a woman who sat in a huge old oak tree for weeks because she did not believe the tree should be cut down. That sounded odd to me until I read the entire article. Developers wanted to cut down the tree and put a building in its place. She was passionate about preserving the history of her town, and saving that historic tree was significant to her. Evidently, she did not mind sacrificing her time and energy, because she felt this was part of her life purpose. It's that passion behind the cause that gives meaning to our lives.

After my sister was diagnosed with breast cancer, not only did her life change, but mine as well. She was a hairdresser and I was a nurse at the time. I was living my passion in the medical field because I liked to help people live healthier lives. My sister's passion was to help people feel good by making them look good. Because of her cancer, my sister's purpose changed. Her health and the health of others became a priority. Looking good was simply a plus. My purpose changed from just helping people live healthier lives to helping them live more fulfilling emotional and spiritual lives, as well as physically healthy lives.

I went back to school to incorporate counseling as part of my purpose. My sister included discussing health issues into her conversations with her clients. Her oft-repeated phrase was, "If you have your health, you have everything." How important is your health to you? Once you lose it, your view of life changes. You realize how good you had it and you work diligently at getting your good health back. This desire can awaken your juices to discover or rediscover your life mission.

*I would much rather have regrets about not doing what people said, than regretting not doing what my heart led me to and wondering what life had been like if I'd just been myself.*

Brittany Renée

## Live your purpose and mission in life

Do you know if you are living your life purpose? You might know it instantly or you might have no idea. You are usually living your purpose if you feel good about where you are in your life. You like what you do and who you are. By being in sync with your life purpose, you make your decisions according to your values and experience harmony within your life.

Do you believe you are accomplishing your mission in life right now? Some of us do not give much thought to what our mission in life is. We just live our lives from day to day. Usually we get up and go to work, put in eight hours, and when we get home we put in more hours doing household chores and other obligations. Everyone has their normal routine.

Most companies and agencies have mission statements that focus on their creed or philosophy. These businesses want you (the customer or client) to know that their foremost purpose is to make your experience more enjoyable and one to remember. After all, their goal is to get your business again. What if you had a mission statement? An actual statement that helps you identify with your purpose. A statement that tells others who you are and what you stand for as you live your life purpose.

If you don't have one, try reading mission statements of various products and notice how they identify the purpose of the product.

Examples:

- Shampoo: to hydrate and nourish hair
- Lotion: to enrich and heal sensitive skin
- Lip balm: to heal and protect lips
- Air Freshener: to enhance your home and create a more inviting atmosphere.

Of course your mission statement would describe your purpose, and it would be personal and unique to you. *Have a statement that defines who you are and what you stand for.* This statement should include your morals and values. Some people think it is easier for companies or agencies to write mission statements about their services than it is for a person to write a unique mission statement. Most of us don't even think about what our mission in life entails.

A friend of mine, Steve, owns his own landscaping business. One day as he was checking my sprinkler system, I asked him how he was doing. His answer was, "Everything is going great." He seemed genuinely happy and told me that his mission in life is to make people happy. He said that if he makes his customers' yards look good, they will be happy and that makes him happy. His job is not an easy one, but what a clear-cut mission statement.

Another friend, Deborah, is a flight attendant. Her life mission is, as she says, "to keep her passengers comfortable" while they are on their flight. She truly loves her job and constantly thinks of ways to better assist passengers. She has a unique way with her smile and conversations, and that does make her passengers feel comfortable.

When I took a flight several years ago, a very nice flight attendant gave me a bottle of champagne as I was departing the plane. I had not complained about anything during the trip, but I had told her how pleasant she had made my journey. I guess she gave the champagne to me as a gesture of thanks, and I have not forgotten her kindness. She seemed to be passionate about her job, and I believe her life mission was to show appreciation to others in caring ways.

Your mission statement highlights your life purpose. According to Stephen Covey, your mission statement is your expression of your innermost values and guidelines. Your personal mission statement should be a statement that when others hear or read it, they say, "Yes, that's who you are!" And more importantly, you should totally believe it, and it needs to personify your beliefs and values. Yours, not someone else's!

How do you know what a certain company's mission statement is? Most companies have their mission statement displayed on a wall where it can be easily seen. Some companies print it in their brochures. Why? Because a company's mission statement is a reflection of its beliefs and values. Many of us choose who we do business with according to our morals and values, and if a certain company's values don't coincide with ours, then we can choose another one that does.

Are you living by your mission statement? Do others know what you embrace in life? If you have a specific and clear mission statement, you are more likely to live by it. Many self-improvement experts believe goals are more obtainable if you write them down. In the same manner, if you write down your mission statement, you are more likely to strive to obtain it. Let's look at a few advantages of having a mission statement and writing it down.

- You are able to identify exactly what you want to accomplish with your life.
- Your mission statement is the framework for your character, nature, and outlook in life, as well as the foundation for making important daily decisions and life-changing decisions.
- You are able to live your life more fully, because when situations come along and throw you off track, you will still know what your goals and objectives are.

- You feel more confident in identifying what matters the most to you. What you want to be and do with your life is front and center in your mind.

I'll share my life purpose and mission statement with you. It includes my life philosophy. Perhaps it will help you with yours.

> My life purpose is to inspire others to dream and to pursue those dreams. My mission statement is to guide clients in achieving outstanding results by challenging them to reach their potential and to go beyond their expectations. My philosophy in life is that we have only one life and we should live it to the fullest! Every day is a gift!

All these statements are consistent with the way I live my life. Your mission and life purpose statements should be clear and precise. They can be one or two lines about who you are and what you want to accomplish in life. How will your mission and purpose in life benefit you, benefit others, and glorify God?

## Your unique statement

I've provided you with a few examples of mission statements, and there is more information about the importance of developing a personal and professional mission statement in Mr. Covey's book, *The 7 Habits of Highly Effective People*. I encourage you to read the section on mission statements. He believes it will be easier for you to write a mission statement if you break it down to include all the specific roles you play in your life, both personally and professionally. He has examples that are easy to understand in his book.

Let me give you the "Readers Digest" version of what these examples are. Some personal roles in our lives are spouse, mother, father, sibling, friend, Christian; professional roles are office manager, boss, salesperson, administrator. When developing your mission statement, you can include your specific roles or just one certain role that you like best. Make it a fun, exciting process. Use words that describe you and your views in life. Your mission statement can be revised from time to time as you mature in life. To see if you're on target, share it with your friends while you are working on it and see if they say, "Yes, this is you. It's who you are and what you represent." Think of it as your personal creed that you truly live by.

## It's up to you

To fully enjoy your journey through life, you want to live each day with an inborn desire to accomplish your goals. No one says you have to jump up and down with excitement every moment, but by setting goals and reaching them, you will be doing what you most enjoy. Isn't that what brings you happiness and fulfillment? You must believe that you are completely and unquestionably responsible for your future.

By recognizing and using your life gifts, by being passionate about your life purpose, and by having a mission statement as well as goals for your future, you are well on your way to living a more fulfilled life. Another question to ask is, "How do I see myself?" In the next chapter, we will focus on the importance of envisioning yourself in a certain way. This technique can influence the kind of life you live and who you can become. How you see yourself will influence how others see you and treat you. We will look at the importance of having a specific plan for your life, and whether it's better just to go with the flow.

Remember, reading and absorbing the material is good, but for new habits to form and lasting changes to take hold, you need to actually do the Action Steps. Add more steps of your own that you think will move you forward. So take some uninterrupted quiet time for yourself, as well as a pen and paper, and do the following Action Steps.

## Call to Action Steps:

- Evaluate how you spend your time each day. Do you accomplish the things you set out to do, or do you waste time by doing things that do not make you feel fulfilled or energized? Remember what we said about "busyness." Being busy does not mean accomplishing the things that are most important. Keep a notebook or appointment book close by. Write down the things most important for you to do that day and do them. Forget about the ones that are not that important; you can do them later.

- Think about how you make most of your decisions: through logic (reasoning and analyzing everything), confidence (you feel sure you know best), or emotions or intuition (something inside is trying to tell you something; also known as a gut feeling). If an emotion or intuition is urging you in a certain direction, pay attention. Many times, even our emotions make good decisions. For example: If your neck tenses or your palms become sweaty when you are asked to do something, maybe it is not something you should be doing. Your emotions, through your body, could be telling you that the situation may not be right for you.

- Now that you have spent time thinking about your decision-making process, reevaluate that process. If you make decisions primarily through your emotions (such as when you feel stressed, overwhelmed, guilty, resentful, etc.), you might constantly question your decisions and end up doubting yourself. You need to evaluate these feelings and connect them with your values to better understand the feelings that arise in that moment. You may be unaware of what you're feeling right then, how those feelings are driving your decision making, and make decisions that limit your career and life. Write down your values, review them often, and make your decisions according to your core values. See if your decision-making process improves. With practice, that process can become easier and more effective.

- Do you give your all in everything you do? Do you know what your gifts are? If you already know what your life purpose is, apply it to every area of your life. If you enjoy your home and work life, you are most likely living through your life purpose. You feel passionate about your accomplishments and your life defines who you are. If not, try focusing on what is holding you back. Find different hobbies or interests. Do you enjoy them? Try something new. Do it with the expectation of feeling fulfilled and rewarded.

- Brainstorm ideas. All kinds of ideas—even silly ideas! You never know where it may lead you. Read the story of how Barney, the purple dinosaur, was born. Think like a kid again. What did you dream of doing or being when you were a child? Decide to do something you have never done before. Take a college class of something you think you might enjoy (cooking, pottery, or photography), learn a new sport, or join a club. Look through magazines you don't normally subscribe too. Venture out!

- Write down your suggestions or ideas—no matter how silly. Try some of them and check off the ones that you totally do not like. For the ideas that appeal to you, research them, talk to others who work in that area, see if that is what you would enjoy doing. Start narrowing your focus, eliminating those ideas you thought you would like but didn't after you tried them. Apply this activity to possible jobs. Most of us would like a job that feels like a hobby as we do it. Think of what Confucius said: "Find a job you love and you'll never work a day in your life."

- Ask your friends what they think about your new ideas. They may come up with suggestions that you haven't thought of. Others can tell you things about yourself that you overlooked as being a gift, talent, or skill. Discovering your passion and life purpose is a journey of its own. Don't stress over it; it is meant to be enjoyed. There are many books that can assist you in finding your purpose, if you still need assistance. I like *Become Who You Were Born to Be* by Brian Souza. Review the resource page at the end of this book.

- Write your mission statement. Come up with a specific one that fits your purpose in life. It doesn't need to be a paragraph; a simple one-or two-line statement is fine. Ask your friends and coworkers what they think about your purpose and mission in life. The insight of others who know you well might help you in creating your mission statement. Write it down, look at it often, and evaluate if you are truly living it. Remember that it can be modified from time to time. Start today to live your life through your purpose. You will become more passionate about your life as you begin to accomplish your mission.

PRINCIPLE 5

# Unleash Your Personal Power to Initiate Change as a Bridge for Personal Growth

*Lighten up and turn your flaws into strengths.*

> **The imperfections of a man, his frailties, his faults, are just as important as his virtues. You can't separate them. They're wedded.**
>
> Henry Miller

## Accept that you have flaws

Character flaws can be seen as stepping stones that lead you to the awareness of a better life. These weaknesses allow you to see life in a different way. If you can consider your faults or mistakes as learning experiences instead of weaknesses or failures, you will benefit from them. One of the best ways to gain self-worth and respect is to be humble and admit that you are not perfect. You do not need to be perfect to make it in this world. There's nothing wrong with wanting a flawless life, as long as you realize you are okay as you are.

To some of us, it is so important to have all of the right answers and to do everything perfectly the first time. Otherwise, we think of ourselves as inadequate. We don't like to have flaws, we want everything perfect. Perfect bodies, perfect children, and the perfect job. You know what I mean! The funny thing is, even when you think someone has the perfect job, give them an hour and they will tell you everything wrong with it. Tell a friend how good she looks and she can spout off to you several things right off the bat that are wrong with her! The sooner we realize it's okay to make mistakes or not get everything right the first time, the sooner we can relax and truly live our lives as they were meant to be. Being perfect is overrated! Nothing illustrates this better than the following story.

## The story of two pots

A water bearer had two large pots hanging from the ends of the pole that he carried on his neck. One pot had a crack in it, while the other pot was perfect and always delivered a full load of water. At the end of the long walk from the stream to the master's house, the cracked pot always arrived only half full. This went on for two years, with the water bearer delivering only one and a half pots of water to his master's house every day.

The perfect pot was most proud of its accomplishments, pleased in the design for which it was made. But the poor cracked pot was ashamed of its own imperfection, and miserable that it was unable to accomplish what it had been made to do. After two years of enduring this bitter shame, the cracked pot spoke to the water bearer one day by the stream. "I am ashamed of myself and I apologize to you." "Why?" asked the bearer. "What are you ashamed of?" "I am only able to deliver half my load because this crack in my side causes water to leak out. You have to do all of this work, but because of my flaw, you don't get the full worth from your efforts."

The water bearer felt sorry for the old cracked pot, and in his compassion he said, "As we return to the master's house, I want you to notice the beautiful flowers along the path." As they went up the hill, the cracked pot saw the sun warming the beautiful wild flowers on the side of the path, and was cheered somewhat. But at the end of the trail, the pot still felt the old shame because it had leaked out half its load, and so again it apologized to the bearer for its failure. The bearer asked the pot, "Did you not notice that there were flowers only on your side of the path, and not on the other pot's side? That's because I have always known about your flaw, and I took advantage of it. I planted flower seeds on your side of the path, and every day while we've walked back from the stream, you have watered them. For two years I have been able to pick these beautiful flowers to decorate my master's table. Without you being just the way you are, he would not have this beauty to grace his house."[1]

We all have flaws or weaknesses. Maybe we should think of ourselves as "cracked pots"! And instead of dwelling on how your imperfections inhibit you, think of ways to take advantage of them. It's important to realize your weaknesses so you can turn them into strengths. If we will allow, Jesus will use our flaws to grace His Father's table. In God's eyes nothing goes to waste. Remember, "God doesn't make junk!"

Don't be afraid of your flaws. You may have imperfections, but you can use them for your benefit. Be creative and figure out ways you can turn them into something useful. Think of Dumbo. Others made fun of him because of his huge ears, but after he used them to fly, he no longer felt defective. He became powerful. Life is a gift and each day has its own treasures and surprises, so try to see the good in everything. Accept no excuses, especially from yourself!

## Do a reality check

*I myself am made entirely of flaws, stitched together with good intentions.*

Augusten Burroughs

What you consider your character flaws others may see as your strengths. If you are shy, you might feel weak because you do not speak up as much as others do. Others, however, may see your quietness as deliberation because you are probably a good listener. The art of listening is a powerful tool, and others probably wish they could be more like you. Or are you opinionated? Maybe you were denied the right to speak your mind when you were growing up, and now you feel it is most important for you to express your opinions and beliefs. Someone may consider you assertive because you are determined to talk about your viewpoints. So use your flaws to your advantage, turn your weaknesses into strength.

Our faults and not-so-admirable traits can be a hindrance at times. You can acquire a negative trait because of a situation you have no control over. How much influence did, or does, your environment have on your personal development? Judgmental parents could have caused you to be stubborn and set in your ways, or it could have helped you to be creative and optimistic. Even if you believe you are set in your ways, you can still flip around your flaws and turn them into positive traits.

If you allow your flaws or weaknesses to overtake you, you might end up playing the role of a victim. The victim sees himself as at the mercy of others. He is damaged, hurt, or suffering. He can't conceive of doing any better than he is now. Thinking like that will definitely create problems. If your character flaw has caused harm to you or others and you feel bad or frustrated about it, consider your uncomfortable feelings as a catalyst for change. You can change. You will change—for the better! So seize the opportunity to reevaluate your faults by keeping their positive aspects and letting go of the negative.

Work on improving the part that prevents you from being in charge of your life. Start with self-awareness. Realize how you deal with that trait and how it affects your relationship with others. What I mean is, notice when you use this trait (flaw). Do you use it when it is useful or when it is detrimental to you or others? For example, are you a perfectionist? In some aspects, this can be a positive if your job is one in which you need to be organized and always on top of things. In relationships, though, it could be damaging because you might critique others with whom you socialize, judging them unfairly for their lack of perfection. This puts your relationships in jeopardy. Make a conscious effort not to be overly focused in every area of your life. Try to relax and let go of the need to be perfect.

I am inspired when I read stories about compassionate and caring people. One particular person is Mother Theresa. She was a saintly woman who always put others needs in front of hers. I've read that when the Vatican investigated her life to decide whether she was a good candidate for canonization, they questioned some of the priests who worked with her. The priests described her as stubborn, controlling, and difficult to work with! That may be true, but these traits are probably what helped her to follow her life's calling to help the poor. She used these faults to her advantage and did more than most of us will do in our lifetime.

Do you think humility is putting others first and taking care of yourself last? Is it important for you to feel powerful, to be the one who has the answer to every situation, and to single-handedly take care of everything so others can live a better or happier life? Doing for others or having all the answers may start out as humility, but can end up turning you into a boasting, proud person, and it can cause burnout. Don't fall into this trap! This behavior could eventually take over your life, allow others to take advantage of you, and you could end up being subservient to others' needs and wants. Before you know it, you will have invested too much of yourself in others, and they will keep asking more of you. Being humble is a great attribute to have, but knowing when to set boundaries is crucial. Step back and allow others to be in charge of their own lives.

There's a Chinese proverb that stresses the importance of helping someone, but not taking over his life. It goes like this: "Give a man a fish and you feed him for a day. Teach a man how to fish and you feed him for a lifetime." In other words, don't enable others to depend on you but help them to help themselves. A humble person accepts he is not perfect and admits he has flaws. He realizes his flaws may lead him to his strengths. A quote by the evangelical minister Rick Warren describes humility pretty well: "Humility is not thinking less of yourself; it's thinking of yourself less."

God sees beyond our faults. If God can accept us with our flaws, why can't we accept ourselves and realize we don't have to be perfect to make it in this world? I've been told before not to look at something for what it is, but for what it can be. Hopefully that's how God looks at us, as we are continually molding ourselves into who we want to be. This is a lifelong process.

*When you make a mistake, don't look back at it long. Take the reason of the thing into your mind and then look forward. Mistakes are lessons of wisdom. The past cannot be changed. The future is yet in your power.*

Hugh White

## Powerlessness vs. humility

Throughout your life you might experience feelings of powerlessness, and that is not always a bad thing. When you recognize that you are powerless to fix the things you need to fix, even when you have tried, new strengths appear. My clients in AA (Alcoholics Anonymous) say that the first thing they learn in the meetings is that they are powerless over alcohol. The need for alcohol makes them feel weak and broken. Powerless, they've hit rock bottom.

Only after they have participated in the 12-step program does the personal growth process begin. The seed of humility is planted, and as it grows, it begins to heal the pain of addiction. And humility can be a great asset for all of us. It teaches us to come down off our high horse and to live a simpler life. Having humility allows you to accept help from others and to return the favor when someone else needs assistance. Why try to do it all by yourself? Just so you can let everyone know how wonderful and self-sufficient you are?

When I think of humility, I think of Jesus. He had more boasting rights than anyone, but He would heal people and tell them not to tell anyone. If that were one of us, we would probably want the credit for that! Think of how famous we would be if we healed someone who was blind or lame. These days so many people want credit for everything they do. They expect acknowledgment and praise, or even a nice newspaper article that spreads the news of how great they are.

You can be your own worst enemy when you refuse to seize opportunities to review your faults and evaluate what you can change for the better. Arrogance or pride can creep in and distract you from the things that really matter the most in your life. Pride keeps you from apologizing when you need to, and it allows greed to take over. On the other hand, through humility you can admit your powerlessness over situations in your life, and you can accept responsibility for your thoughts, behaviors, and actions that are hurtful or damaging to yourself and to others. You are able to take control of your life and work to improve the flaws that are holding you back. Being humble can make you feel powerful as you build on your personal strengths. Always hold yourself accountable for your actions. Admit that you have faults—and then turn them into strengths.

## Build on your strengths

You may think you don't have any strengths, but we all have strengths. We seem to dwell on our weaknesses instead of building up our positive traits or strengths. It is to your advantage to know your strengths as well as your weaknesses. If you are not sure of your strengths, it might be beneficial to take a standardized personality test. You can get an idea of why you act the way you do, and that can help you look for a job or a lifestyle that better fits you. These tests are enlightening and fun. Some are free on the Internet, while some websites may charge a small fee. Assessments such as Myers-Briggs and DISC help people identify their personality traits.

Myers-Briggs uses personality categories. Are you an extravert or introvert? Are you more of a feeling person or a thinking person? By knowing the answers to these questions, you can have greater insight into how you make your decisions and why you may do better working alone instead of being a team player in your job. The DISC personality assessment is based on four basic temperaments that blend together to determine your unique personality. This assessment assists you in understanding why you think the way you do, feel the way you do, and act the way you do. (I sure could have used this information when my children were growing up!) All of us can benefit from taking these tests.

I take the Myers-Briggs assessment called Jung Typology Test on www.humanmetrics.com for free. (There is a fee for other assessments on this site.) In Dr. Robert Rohm's book *Who Do You Think You Are Anyway?*, DISC is presented in an interesting and fun way. He helps you understand the similarities and differences in your temperament, as well as the people with whom you work or associate. It is an easy read; you don't have to be a professional to understand this material. Another great resource I recommend for discovering your strengths is Tom Rath's book *Strengths Finder 2.0*. It shows you what your top five strengths are, among the thirty-four they evaluate. It is also easy to read and understand. It will assist you in finding your strengths and ways you can apply them daily. If you're determined to change, these tests reveal who you are. As the great baseball coach Yogi Berra said, "If you don't know where you are going, you might wind up somewhere else." These assessments help you get to the right place.

## Strength or weakness

Dave Meyer, author of *The Sage and Scholars Guide of Coaching Assessments*, suggests that when you overuse your strengths, you turn them into weaknesses. One of your strengths might be organizational abilities, which can be a benefit at work. But what if you can't relax at home until everything is in its place? You will always feel as if you have to pick up after others or rearrange your belongings, and this becomes tiresome and can irritate others. What if you do this organizing at other places and people are offended by it? That's when your skill or ability becomes a weakness or hindrance.[2]

Do you remember that in a previous chapter we discussed how everyone has a spiritual gift(s)? Can you overuse them until they too disrupt your life? If you have the gift of mercy and you stay busy helping others to the point that you neglect yourself or your family, then the gift becomes a burden. If you fill your day with the concerns and needs of others, how does it make you feel? You may feel satisfied, blessed, and powerful; or you may feel stressed, overwhelmed, and taken advantage of. What if you are tired of your days being filled with chores and errands for others? There are many people in the working world who labor endlessly because they do not want to delegate, afraid that other people's work won't be done to their standards! Everybody knows a person like this. The point is, you need to feel good about yourself and what you are doing. Otherwise, it will wear you down and cause you to resent what your life or job has become.

## Denise's story

Forty-three-year-old Denise felt depressed, believing she had no control over her time or her life. She was always at the beck and call of her mother. Her mother, elderly and a widow, was constantly phoning Denise, telling her of her needs. Denise felt she had to do everything her demanding mother wanted when she wanted it. She could not tell her mother no, even though she wanted to desperately. She put her life on hold in order to fulfill her mother's constant demands, believing that if she didn't, she would not be a good daughter. She had lived this way for most of her life and never realized it did not have to be like that. After we discussed the importance of setting boundaries, when to say yes and when to say no, she understood that she had a choice and that her decisions didn't determine whether she was a good daughter or not. Denise could be in charge of her life again!

Denise began to realize that she was neglecting her needs and values by always accommodating her mother. Her previous beliefs had been limiting and self-defeating, and now she viewed her situation differently. Once we reframed the situation, she realized she would still be living up to her values if she placed limitations on what and when she could do things for her mother.

We came up with a way for Denise to talk with her mother and inform her that she could no longer do everything her mother demanded because she had a life of her own. Denise told her mother that she would not do things for her daily, but once a week she would pick her up and they could spend the entire day together getting things accomplished.

Denise realized she could say no without feeling guilty, and she could use other family members and resources to assist with her mother's care. Her mother stopped asking her to tend to her every need and became more independent by doing some things herself. Denise realized how important it was to be aware of her values and to live by them in a way that moved her toward her goals and dreams. Denise and her mother now respect each other in a different way. They can be honest with each other and express their true feelings without fear of rejection. Denise's strength of dedication and responsibility, which she had allowed to become a weakness, was once again a valued strength.

## Activate your personal power

In the above story, Denise relinquished her strength. She gave up her personal power. She lost that inner awareness that made her feel in control of her life. She indeed felt powerless. What about you? Are you entangled in a situation that drains your energy and makes you fearful? If so, this is the time to activate your personal power, that inner awareness that can make you feel in control of your life. The feeling deep down inside you that says you can overcome this situation. When Denise realized the situation with her mother made her feel powerless, she was able to step back, evaluate, and resolve the situation to both her and her mom's benefit. Remember, powerlessness is only in control if you let it be.

## How do I know when to let go?

My vision for my life was to get married, have children, and be a nurse. I did all three and life was good. The situations in my life were no different from anyone else's until I went through a divorce after being married for twenty-three years. I was devastated because I wanted my children to have a mom and dad living under the same roof. My parents had divorced when I was young, and I was determined that my marriage was going to be different. No matter what happened, we would be able to work it out. Sometimes things just don't work out the way we think they should. This was a roadblock that caused a major detour in my life. But as bad as it was going through a divorce, I think God was preparing me for what I would go through next.

I had always been the type of person who could handle anything, not let any circumstances stop me from going after my goals. God has a way of teaching us to trust Him, to lean on Him and stop trying to handle things on our own. I learned that the hard way!

Three months after my divorce, one of my younger sisters was diagnosed with breast cancer. It was in an advanced stage. God tells us that He will not put us through more than we can bear. Normally I believed Him, but now my fears were taking over, and I didn't know if I could handle what was ahead of me. All I could do for my sister was accompany her to her chemo treatments and give her moral support. After she had gone through several treatments, she was feeling depressed about her health situation and seemed close to giving up. My heart was burdened for her, for our family, and for myself. I felt totally powerless, and one day at work I felt an overwhelming sadness in my heart. I couldn't focus on my work. As I was walking to my desk, I noticed a piece of paper taped on a counter. Out of curiosity, I walked over and read it. It said: Be still and know that I am God. Those eight words hit me like a ton of bricks, and I realized instantly that I needed to stop trying to be in charge of the situation and give it to God. Something was telling me that at a time like this, when I had no control, it was okay to feel powerless.

When my sister was first diagnosed, I felt I had to be in control and fix everything. After all, I was a nurse and nurses make people well. But after I read that Bible verse, a big weight was lifted off my shoulders. I decided to pray more and realize that there is someone much greater and more powerful than I looking after my sister, myself, and our family. The realization that God was in charge was so powerful, it helped me to see things differently. My sister's life, mine, and my family's lives were all put on hold while she went through her treatment. Her illness taught all of us how precious life was and how blessed we were to have another day together. Going through this ordeal changed the course of my life as well as my sister's. What we had envisioned for ourselves was not what God had planned for us. Our priorities of what was, and was not, important changed forever because of that experience.

Because I'd been through a divorce and helped my sister face her illness, my life had changed. I began to think about a new game plan for my life, as my purpose was different now. I asked God often what he wanted me to do with my life, because I no longer felt in control of it. I wasn't sure what or where my path was headed, but I decided to follow Him instead of trying to be the leader. God had my full attention! It was actually comforting to know that I did not have to face this life crisis on my own. I had always had faith in God, but it had never been tested to this extreme.

## It pays to listen

Have you heard the story about the man who almost drowned because he was waiting on God to save him? A heavy rain came down, and everyone was leaving their homes to go to a safe shelter. One man was standing on his front porch, and a neighbor asked him if he wanted a ride in his truck to get to the shelter. "No," the man said. "God will provide." As the water was rising, another man came by in a boat and told the man to get in or he might drown. The man refused, saying, "No, God will provide." Finally, a helicopter flew over his house and the pilot saw the man on his roof. He yelled at him and told him he would throw him a rope. The man could grab it and be lifted up into the helicopter. The man refused, still believing that God would provide. Of course, the man drowned. When he met Peter at the pearly gates, Saint Peter said, "For crying out loud, mister, God sent a truck, a boat, and a helicopter! What did you expect?"

We laugh at the story, but how many times have we done the same thing? Opportunities come our way, but we ignore them or we refuse to think of them as opportunities. We get set in our ways and think things should be done our way only. What if our way leads us on the same beaten path to nowhere? Do you ever feel like you are being swept along on a busy interstate, but you're afraid to get off because it might be the wrong exit? The idea of changing things is scary, but at least it allows you to explore different options. You can travel roads that you have never been down before, and it could be the best decision you ever made. The desire to see things differently is the beginning of change.

*Life isn't about finding yourself. Life is about creating yourself.*

George Bernard Shaw

## Change is easy, right? Wrong!

Knowing who you are and what you want out of life is important, but to experience a "new and improved" life outwardly, you will need to change things inwardly first. In order for you to reap the benefits of a more satisfying and fulfilling life, it is essential for you to realize that something's got to be done differently. The process of change can be intimidating, challenging, and rewarding all at the same time. But if you want something badly enough, you will do what it takes to get it. How many times have you been told that if you don't like a situation, do something to change it? I don't know about you, but if I don't want to change something, I can come up with fifty excuses as to why change is not a good idea. In our minds the pathway to changing something is too rough, thorny, or complicated. Especially if it involves changing something about ourselves!

Most of us prefer for someone else to change so we can stay the way we are. It's easy to convince ourselves that it's the other person, group, or agency that needs to change its ways. Let me illustrate. If you are a church-going person, you know how difficult it is to change things within the church community. After I had my three sons, I decided it was time we changed the time for church services. Nine o'clock in the morning was just too early for me to have myself and all three children dressed and ready for church. Much less to be on time! I approached some of the leaders of the church about changing the time to one hour later. Surely they would agree with me after I explained to them why it needed to be changed. I might as well been talking to a wall. The answer was, absolutely not! When I asked why, the response was, "Because we've always done it this way." This answer drives me crazy because it tells me that it's an excuse. Leaving things as they are is much easier than stirring up a hornet's nest by trying to change things, which leads us to discussing change and the change cycle.

There are thousands of books written about change, and I feel it is just one of the principles that is crucial to living a more satisfying and fulfilling life. If you prefer not to change either yourself or situations in your life, you will have to accept that where you are and what you are right now is the best you can ever expect.

It takes a lot of effort to change, whether it is your appearance, your environment, your relationships, or your mindset. You must first face the fact that if you are not happy with yourself or satisfied with the way things are, you are the one who needs to do something about it. One of my mottos is "Dream It, Believe It, Do It"—because all three components are necessary for you to be the kind of person you want to be and to live the kind of life you desire and deserve. Let's talk about how to do it.

*Never give up, for that is just the place and time that the tide will turn.*

Harriet Beecher Stowe

## The Change Cycle

## Step 1: Acknowledge the problem

The process of change begins with recognizing the problems and situations that drain you. Know that you do not need to tolerate the things that are not moving you forward. If they are not for you, they must be against you! Change begins with you being dissatisfied with something about you or about your life. Mentally accepting that you are ready to face certain situations and to do whatever is needed to change begins the *Change Cycle*. Having a positive belief in yourself and your abilities is most empowering. Repeat positive sayings to yourself as you write down the changes you want to accomplish. Remember, you are what you think.

## Step 2: Envision the change

The next step is to imagine or envision how the changes will benefit you. By visualizing the results, rewards, or benefits you will receive from this step in the *Change Cycle,* your motivation to succeed will intensify. When you begin experiencing the results—such as freedom to be yourself, more respect, a job you love, improved health—your commitment to your dreams and goals will surge. There will be no stopping you. You will believe and know that you are worth every effort you make and every struggle you face as you continue through the *Change Cycle*. Try using this statement often during your change process to remind you of your potential benefits: "I am imagining living my life without [people who drain me, worrying about finances, living in a messy home, etc.]." Think of the benefits you'll receive, and changing things in your life will become easier. Don't let others interfere with your dreams. It's your world!

## Step 3: Be committed and stay dedicated

It's great to have a positive mindset and to envision your results, but without the commitment and dedication to actually do the things that need to be done, you might as well put your thoughts in a box and bury them. Talk is cheap, so you must "talk the talk and walk the walk" in order to succeed in the *Change Cycle*. You will learn to unleash your potential and embrace the new challenges you encounter. Find a way to see your new challenges as opportunities or stepping stones that move you closer to your goals. Gain from each trial something that could eventually steer you to the next best possible solution for your circumstances. Every time you face the consequences of changing you or something in your life, stay committed and determined by saying to yourself, "Bring it on!" Totally believe that nothing is too difficult for you to do.

## Step 4: Achieve powerful results

This step is the culmination of the process, seeing your goals and dreams become reality. You will accomplish things that you never thought you could. Get to know your values and realize that you are the one setting your priorities and the boundaries that make sense to you. You are able to make your own decisions and not worry about what others think or say. Having a level of confidence that provides inner peace and security allows you to experience unlimited success and happiness. Now you can appreciate and celebrate the power within you—the power to make a difference.

Hopefully this *Change Cycle* will motivate you to make the changes necessary for you to live a more fulfilling life. Don't procrastinate. Making changes can be exciting and refreshing. Think of it as redecorating your life, like putting a fresh coat of paint on your walls (having a new attitude), or rearranging your furniture to make your room look bigger (exposed to more opportunities). Once you get started and take the first step, the process becomes easier and results begin to flow. There is no limit to what you can accomplish or become. Pick a specific change strategy that fits your need and be ready to reap the benefits.

Before I get off my soapbox about the importance of change, I would like to share one more simple analysis that has helped many of my clients think differently about the process and benefits of changing. It was written by Portia Nelson and is titled *Autobiography in Five Short Chapters*. I have taken the liberty to paraphrase it here. It's a simple story but it illustrates the phases you must deal with in order to change yourself and any situation in your life—if you choose to do so.

## The Hole

Ms. Nelson describes life change through the illustration of a person who walks down a street and falls into a deep hole in the sidewalk. Each time the person falls in he feels helpless yet doesn't think he has a problem. This correlates with the person who constantly thinks that they don't have a problem and don't need to change.

So what does this lead to? The person decides to pretend that the hole isn't really there! As he walks down the same sidewalk guess what? He falls in again! This time he realizes maybe he does need to change, but he lacks the commitment or dedication to do it.

This lack of commitment leads to the person falling into the hole on purpose. Why? The same reason that most of us keep doing what we're doing and getting nowhere. It's a pattern, a habit! And it's a habit that's hard to break. You may have created the circumstances that put you in the situation but you're beginning to realize that you can choose to change. Now you can begin to develop new insights and decide to do something about "the hole."

The last two chapters are refreshing because you decide to start a new chapter in your life. You are in charge and it's your decision to change things. So you weigh the other possibilities to see how best to respond to the problem in a different manner. So as in our story, there's a hole in the sidewalk; I keep falling into the hole every time I walk down the street. What can I do? I can walk on the other side of the street but that simply pretends the problem isn't there. I've got it! Think I'll try another route and walk down a different street!

Sounds all too simple but it's not until you break out of your old pattern of thinking and living. Walking down a different street means you are now engaged in the process of changing yourself or your situation. You are able to see yourself and your life differently. You no longer think about your old ways. Congratulations!

Once change takes place, you will discover things about yourself that you never knew before. You will feel more comfortable being yourself. Your confidence and self-satisfaction will allow you to express yourself in a million ways. Your reality is one that you create.

Although this is the end of the change process, it is important to do a periodic maintenance check. It is so easy to go back to your old nonproductive ways, but you have worked too diligently to get where you are now. It's the same as if you were on a strict diet and lost the amount of weight you wanted to lose. Then for no apparent reason, you go back to your old way of eating that put on the weight originally. Just because you have achieved the results you wanted is not a green light to go back to your old habits. If you do, your weight will creep back up and you will have to start the process all over again. Same street, same hole, same result.

*We don't laugh because we're happy—we're happy because we laugh.*

William James

## Lighten up

Don't take life so seriously! Lighten up and add humor as you go through your transformation process. Humor brings a balance that helps us get through the chaotic times in our lives. Sometimes it's just as easy to laugh as to cry. Someone once told me that being able to laugh at yourself, or having the ability to lighten up, is equivalent to having shock absorbers on a car. He explained it this way.

Shock absorbers on a car minimize the jolts and vibrations, so when you hit a pothole or a rough spot in the road, you won't bounce all over the road. Shock absorbers make it safer for you to drive and help you enjoy a more comfortable ride. If not for shock absorbers, you could lose control of the car if you hit a bad patch of road and have a serious accident. Lastly, he told me that shock absorbers decrease the wear and tear on your car because they absorb most of the force from road bumps and keep the frame from being damaged.

He then asked me to think about what laughter can do for me as I go about living my life. He pointed out that by taking things lightly, or even simply smiling or laughing, causes our brains to release the feel-good endorphins that decrease feelings of anxiety, grief, depression, irritation, and anger. In other words, laughter is a powerful source of health and well-being. What I gathered from his comparison was that if a person can develop a sense of humor and not take life too seriously, his life can be more fulfilling and enjoyable. He can accept whatever comes his way, knowing he can handle it. Having a sense of inner peace lessens the jolts and helps you avoid the bombs coming your way. You become more resilient as your well-developed sense of humor acts as the shock absorbers for your life.

A sense of humor inspires you to face your challenges, and it allows you to feel safe while being in charge of your life. With a sense of humor, you can handle any unexpected situations and come out smiling. I worked in the medical field for many years and saw firsthand how humor and laughter improved the immune system. Laughter has a lot to do with the mind-body relationship and often really can be the best medicine. During stressful times, humor can change the way you view situations.

Years ago, my youngest son's Christmas wish was for fifty cents. He was four or five years old and kept telling me, "I sure hope I get fifty cents for Christmas." I asked him why he wanted this money, and his reply was, "Because I want to buy a Coke out of the Coke machine." (This was quite a few years ago.) He wanted his own can of soda and he wanted to buy it! I laughed and thought how such a simple request and statement could take away stress and frustration. Aim to add humor to your life daily and be ready to experience its benefits.

No man is an island. We all have certain friends we love to be around because they make us feel good. It is easy to forget about your problems when you laugh and joke with others. So it's beneficial to include those special people in your life-changing process. Let them know what your goals are; when you reach your goals, they can celebrate with you. If you are having difficulties with a situation and are out of solutions, ask your friends for their ideas. It is to your advantage to have others on your side. Being held accountable by your friends also helps you to be more responsible as you reach your goals, and prevents you from backsliding. Friends are always there for you, give you honest answers, and have your best interests at heart. Use them wisely and well.

> *None of us is defined by our circumstances, nor are we defined by how other people perceive us. It is up to each one of us to define ourselves, and that is a life's work. Each of us has the ability to lead a dynamic life by pursuing our unique goals and dreams. There are no limits to what you can do.*
>
> Stedman Graham

Now let's take time to evaluate which direction you are headed in your life. If it's not the direction you've chosen or desire, then there's no better time than now to take the necessary actions to change it. Reflect on the things you can change and don't waste your time on the things you have no control over. Change doesn't just happen. You need to put forth time and effort to make it happen. Take charge!

## Call to Action Steps:

- How effective are you in managing your life? Be aware of your strengths and your flaws. Take a sheet of paper or use space in this book to write down ten (or more) of your strengths. Strengths can be your skills, talents, or positive traits. Examples: friendly and positive with other people, honest, respectful of others, able to fix things, self-disciplined. Review the list often and add more strengths as you grow in your personal development.

Write down your flaws (those things that don't work to your advantage). Examples: talking too much, not taking action, not listening, desire to be perfect in everything, the inability to say no. Find ways to decrease your flaw list by turning your flaws into strengths. If that's not possible, get rid of the flaw permanently. Consult with others for suggestions for eliminating certain flaws.

- Constantly use your strengths and talents. Apply your strengths to areas of your life that you care about, as well as those areas you would like to improve or would like to be more successful. Your strengths will help you reach your goals, meet your everyday needs, and bring more satisfaction and happiness to all areas of your life.

- Don't live as a victim—live as a survivor. View your life as experiences to be treasured instead of continuous problems to be solved. When you live as a victim, you feel powerless and stuck in a rut. Practice reframing your situations to see what you can do differently. Write down the challenging things you are facing. Make a list of three positive things that could come from a difficult situation.

  For example: Your doctor had told you that your blood pressure is high and you may need to go on medication. Take positive things from this, such as:

  1. think of it as an opportunity to take better care of yourself;

  2. eat a more healthy diet;

  3. begin an exercise regimen.

Reframe your situation by thinking differently about it. By doing so, you will become more aware of your inner strengths and gifts and feel more powerful in taking charge of your life.

- Begin the *Change Cycle* now. Look at what you are doing that is not working and do the opposite. Instead of attacking others verbally, decide to listen attentively before you speak. If you are a judgmental and critical person, try being empathetic and more understanding. Change won't happen overnight, but the more you are aware of your not-so-good thoughts and behaviors, the more quickly you can start to alter these habits. One small change leads to bigger changes.

  For example: You want to be more self-confident at work. You don't like the way you are treated by your coworkers, but you are afraid to speak out about it.

  1. Think back to a time when you were confident. What did you do then? Remember how it felt when you were confident.

  2. Practice stating your thoughts/feelings in front of a mirror at home about a situation that's bothering you until you feel comfortable expressing yourself. Then practice saying it to a friend and do role playing with your friend. Frame your statements in a positive way and sound confident as you say them.

  3. Remind yourself of the advantages and benefits of being more confident and assertive. Write down the possible consequences or rewards of speaking out in a positive way.

4. Find a positive affirmation that fits you and makes you feel empowered, such as, “If they can do it, so can I” or “I can be anything I want to be.”

- Recognize when a change strategy is not working and find another approach. What works for one person may not work for another. Don’t give up! Talk with others about the situation or part of your life you are trying to change. They may have ideas or suggestions that you haven’t thought of. It can be as simple as reading books about how others accomplished feats in their lives. Evaluate your progress often to see if you are reaching your goals. If not, change your strategy again.

- Find humor and don’t take life so seriously. When faced with a challenge, it is just as easy to laugh as it is to cry. Sometimes our best ideas come when we are joking around, letting go of our fears and insecurities. Develop your sense of humor and you’ll be more creative with your ideas. You’ll also be more productive, a better communicator, and a better friend. Ways to lighten up are:

    1. Laugh at yourself. Stop expecting to be perfect and plan on making mistakes. You can learn through your bloopers!

    2. Stop and smell the roses. Make yourself laugh heartily (belly laugh) at least once daily. Trainers say a deep belly laugh burns fat! (Another advantage of laughter.)

    3. Watch a comedy movie or read a joke book. Go to a comedy show. There are also plenty of funny sitcoms on television you can watch.

4. Be known as the friend who makes people laugh. When you give gifts, consider a funny card or a humorous book.

Repeat the Serenity Prayer often: *"God, grant me the serenity to accept the things I cannot change; courage to change the things I can; and wisdom to know the difference."*

Reinhold Niebuhr

PRINCIPLE 6

# Create and Design Your Life Story

*Be true to yourself, "walk the walk," and experience inner peace.*

> **Your life is the sum result of all the choices you make, both consciously and unconsciously. If you can control the process of choosing, you can take control of all aspects of your life. You can find the freedom that comes from being in charge of yourself.**
>
> Robert F. Bennett

Your mind is a powerful thing. It can think what it wants to when it wants to. It can even decide if it wants to be positive or negative. Yep, your mind has an attitude, and it can make or break you. The good thing is, *you* are in control of your mind! Your life journey is being written, and it is determined by your experiences (good and bad). Or is it? Charles Swindoll said, "I am convinced that life is 10% what happens to me and 90% how I react to it. And so it is with you . . . we are in charge of our attitudes." Mr. Swindoll is suggesting that how you react or respond to your life happenings greatly influence your outlook on life.

The following story illustrates how it's up to you to use your life experiences to your advantage. The author is unknown, and it is titled "The Law of the Garbage Truck."

## The law of the garbage truck

One day a man hopped into a taxi and the taxi driver took off for the airport. They were driving in the right lane when a car sped out of a parking place right in front of them. The taxi driver slammed on his breaks and skidded, missing the other car by inches. The driver of the other car whipped his head around, yelling at them and making obscene gestures. The taxi driver just smiled and waved at the guy. The passenger asked him why he was being friendly and nice when the other driver could have ruined his car and sent them both to the hospital.

The taxi driver explained that many people were like garbage trucks. They run around full of garbage, full of frustration, full of anger, and full of disappointment. As their garbage piled up, they needed a place to dump it and sometimes they'd dump it on a stranger! "You don't take it personally," the driver said. "Just smile, wave, wish them well, and move on. Don't take their garbage and spread it to other people, at work, at home, or on the streets. Successful people do not let garbage trucks take over their day."

Life is too short to wake up in the morning with regrets, so love the people who treat you right and pray for the ones who don't. And remember, life is 10 percent what you make it and 90 percent how you take it. Attitude is everything.

*Attitude is a little thing that makes a big difference.*

Winston Churchill

## Your attitude is your perception

Do you have a "it's my way or the highway" attitude? Do you believe you are always right and everyone else is wrong? It usually takes a life crisis for people with this type of attitude to even entertain the idea of changing it. But an event such as the death of a loved one, loss of a job, diagnosis of a terminal illness, or a divorce can trigger an attitude overhaul. While going through difficult times, you suddenly see things differently and your priorities change. These stressful situations can shift the direction of your life journey. You may have no control over the situation, but you can control how it affects your present and future life.

*Experience is not what happens to a man; it is what a man does with what happens to him.*

Aldous Huxley

Are you a victim of your own behavior? It is easy to blame others or the circumstances in our lives for our personal unhappiness. Can you remember a time when something bad happened to you because of your own behavior, but you blamed it on someone else? Do you frequently see yourself as a victim and seek to blame others for your failings? This pattern is called not taking responsibility for your actions.

Some people love sympathy. They love to talk about their misery and how badly they are treated. It is easier for them to blame others than to face life's challenges or to search within themselves for the source of their unhappiness. Telling others their hard luck stories produces pity and reinforces their thinking that no one really expects them to be responsible for their own mistakes. These people make it clear that it is someone else's responsibility to make them happy.

## Julian's story

Nineteen-year-old Julian sought counseling because he didn't know what he wanted to do with his life. He felt he wasn't moving forward. He didn't know what he wanted to major in at college. He had failed some of his previous classes and was not interested in his present classes. He worked a part-time job and didn't enjoy it. He was afraid of being fired because that had happened to him before. Overall, Julian was not happy with himself. He thought of himself as a failure—especially in his parents' eyes. Yet in spite of all that, he believed that he had done his part and that family and society had failed him.

In counseling, he told me that he preferred to blame others because it was easier to quit something when it was someone else's fault. Filled with self-pity, Julian was a passive bystander in his own life. He saw only the negatives in his life. And seeing only the negatives provided him with an "out" to justify his behavior.

Over a period of time, we discussed Julian's part in his situation. Could his attitude about life being unfair play a major part in the consequences he was facing? We reframed Julian's situation by discussing what advantages he had that others didn't: his parents paid for his college, he was allowed to live at home rent free, and he'd gotten his job because his parents were friends with his boss.

Through our talks, Julian decided he was being unfair to his parents and his boss by blaming them for his inadequacies and failures. He realized it was time for him to grow up and take responsibility for his inactions and start being proactive in his life.

After a few months of exploring what skills and talents Julian had—but which he didn't realize were skills and talents—he began to see himself in a different way. He realized he was an average college kid who needed to focus on different options available to him. He learned how to relax and make needed changes. He picked college courses that interested him instead of taking what he thought would be easy. By doing these things, he discovered he actually liked being committed and dedicated to his schooling and to his job while he was "finding" the new Julian. He felt stronger both by making his own decisions and by taking the blame if things didn't work out in his favor. No more blaming others! When he accomplished a goal, he rewarded himself. In the end, he changed the way he reacted to situations and began to see the positive in them instead of always the negative. From changing the way he views himself and his life, Julian is a much happier person.

## Practice what you preach

In *The 7 Habits of Highly Effective People*, Stephen Covey brings out a good point when he says you cannot "maintain wholeness" if you do not practice what you preach. In other words, if you do not talk the talk and walk the walk, you lose credibility with others. Your attitude and your behavior are supposed to complement each other in order for you to have balance in life. When you become angry about something, is it natural to suppress that anger? No! Many people do, however, because they choose not to confront the issue that has angered them. They don't want others to think less of them, so they hold things in until they eventually explode.

Does this describe you at times? Not feeling confident enough to say what you truly feel? Too worried of what others will think of you? Afraid of how someone might react if you say what you really want to say? By holding back and not expressing your beliefs, you give away your values of integrity, honesty, and authenticity. For someone to tell you that you are truly a genuine person is a sincere compliment. It means you don't veer from your principles and values. You give answers through your actions—meaning that if you say you will do something, you do it!

When you give up your right to state your feelings honestly, you lose integrity and validity with yourself and with others. People wonder if you really will do what you say you will. If you don't stand firm in your beliefs, certain emotions—such as, doubt, anger, resentment—will creep in, interfere with, and take over the way you live your life. Even positive thoughts turn into negatives, and you stop believing in yourself. This cycle coincides with the inner-fear-ences you store in your brain. It hinders your personal and professional confidence, and the only way to rebuild your confidence is to start making choices based on firm values. Just as with Julian, you must do this in order to take back your life.

## The butterfly story

"The Butterfly Story" reveals different views about the struggles and benefits we can experience in life as a result of certain changes we face. The results are not entirely up to us. Timing and patience play big parts as well.[1]

A man found a cocoon of a butterfly. One day a small opening appeared, and he sat and watched for several hours as the butterfly struggled to force its body through the little hole. Then it seemed to stop making any progress. It appeared stuck. The man decided to help the butterfly, and with a pair of scissors he cut open the cocoon. The butterfly emerged easily, but something was strange. The butterfly had a swollen body and shriveled wings. The man watched the butterfly, expecting it to take on its correct proportions, but nothing changed.

The butterfly stayed the same. It was never able to fly. In his kindness and haste, the man did not realize that the butterfly's struggle to get through the small opening of the cocoon was nature's way of forcing fluid from the body of the butterfly into its wings, so that it would be ready for flight. Like the sapling that grows strong from being buffeted by the wind, in life we all need to struggle sometimes in order to get stronger.

Nobody likes facing struggles, because then their lives are never the same. But afterward you see the need to do something different or better with your life. Others can try to encourage you, but if you are not ready to take action, change won't work. You won't change or even attempt to, so you see encouragement as nagging or forcing you to do something you don't want to do. Only when you decide it's time to spread your wings and fly does change occur. You have to want it bad enough before you invest the energy to take the first step.

*There are three kinds of people in this world: those who make things happen, those who watch things happen, and those who wonder what happened.*

Anonymous

## Break the cycle

When is a good time to begin change? Now! Before a major event happens. Not afterwards, because by then it may be too late. It's like asking the question, "When is the best time to worry about a heart attack?" Before the heart attack, not afterwards! Why wait until a life-threatening event to begin taking care of yourself? Sadly, though, many people do.

From my experience, there are two main reasons why people decide to change: either they are inspired by someone or they feel miserable. That is true for most of us. Reflect back to a time in your life when something moved you to make an important change. It could be a certain movie, book, or song, or perhaps something your spouse, parents, or coworkers did that positively influenced your life decisions.

People like Chris Gardner (*Pursuit of Happyness*) inspire me. Mr. Gardner was an average man who became a single father and homeless. He hit rock bottom. Fortunately, earlier he had stepped out of his comfort zone and asked a very successful man (whom he didn't know) a few questions. That one event helped him on his search for a new life. He was ready and willing to change, and his life is totally different today. A motivational speaker and philanthropist, he shares his challenges with others to encourage them to break the cycle they're in and become who they are meant to be. Chris Gardner is the owner and CEO of Gardner Rich LLC with offices in Chicago, New York, and San Francisco.

Think about times when you were miserable being yourself. Was it because you felt trapped in your life situation? Were you working a dead-end job or involved in a one-way relationship? This happens in marriage often, when one partner is perfectly happy with the way things are while the other partner feels his or her needs don't matter. The one who is miserable will either remain miserable or initiate change.

Maybe you don't enjoy your job but you are the main provider of your family. Perhaps your superiors or coworkers order you around in a harsh manner, and you think you have to take it or you'll get fired. They disregard your abilities or skills and never treat you respectfully. How will you move up the ladder to success in this job? The only way for you to change things is to speak up and do something about the situation. Yes, this is taking a chance, but for change to happen you have to take the initiative. It may not be comfortable, but at least by speaking up you can experience inner peace and perhaps find a confidence you haven't felt before. You stood up and made the choice to change something in your life that was not right. Whatever the consequences, you can face them. And the consequences could turn out to benefit you in ways you never expected. You now know what it feels like to "talk the talk and walk the walk!"

## Create space for inner peace

Joan Borysenko in her book, *Inner Peace for Busy People: 52 Simple Strategies for Transforming Your Life*, believes it's our choice and our decision as to whether we want to practice stress or to practice peace in our everyday lives. When life is complicated, it's easy to forget that you have a choice. When you're constantly bombarded with numerous interruptions, the demands of family life, responsibilities at work, and long to-do lists, it's difficult to feel calm and serene about anything. You forget what it's like to stroll along peacefully and take life as it happens.

Inner peace seems to display itself more easily in the lives of children. It comes out naturally as they enjoy the simple things in life. Can you remember the joy of playing under the water hose on a hot day, licking an ice cream cone as it was melting, or playing with your imaginary friend for hours and not being bored? It's the simple carefree times that usually mean the most to us, less responsibility and no worries. What changes within us as we grow up? What happens to those carefree times and the inner harmony that flowed freely? Have you forfeited your right to live peacefully and to enjoy the simple things by choosing to live a more extravagant and stressful life? If so, it's never too late to reclaim your inner peace.

In my profession, people often tell me that they don't feel a peace from within. They feel they can never be good enough, no matter what they accomplish. They can't let go of past mistakes. When you hang onto resentments or failures, you deny yourself the incredible gift of becoming a better person and living a more fulfilled life. You can't possibly experience all the good that is meant for you, because your energy is wrapped around your insecurities instead of your possibilities. It is important for you to forgive yourself and forgive others. If not, the feelings of resentment, anger, and bitterness will choke the life out of your goals and dreams. No matter what situations you have endured, you can let go of the things that prevent you from living a peaceful life.

Have you ever had a pet that really shouldn't have been a pet, such as a wild squirrel, wild rabbit, or another animal that wasn't meant to be caged? Years ago my younger brother found a baby squirrel that had fallen out of its nest. He was so excited; he wanted to take care of it. He kept it in a cage, fed it warm milk, and held it often. He let the squirrel out of its cage (in the house) for short periods of the day, and it would run up and down his shoulders in excitement. My brother was so proud. After about two months, he decided to take the squirrel outside to see if it could climb a tree. He was sure the squirrel would come back to him, so we siblings went out in the backyard with him to watch this fantastic feat as his squirrel climbed a tree and came back to him. The squirrel took off and climbed up high in the nearest tree, and then jumped to the next tree, and then the next tree, until we couldn't see him anymore. My brother was heartbroken, but he eventually realized that the squirrel was happier doing what was in its nature to do.

This story simplifies what it means to let go of something, especially something you love. Maybe you're hanging onto something that's not meant to be. You could be holding onto something or someone in your life that is preventing you from reaching your full potential. Letting go doesn't mean you have to stop caring, but you need to put things in perspective. My brother's squirrel initially needed extra care and love, but when it could make it on its own, it returned to its natural environment.

Are you holding onto something that is more of a burden than a benefit? Do you feel like you are carrying around a ten-pound weight on your shoulders? If so, you need to reassess the way you are living. Now might be a good time for you to examine your life and let go of certain situations, people, or things that are preventing you from experiencing inner peace. Unnecessary and unfruitful people and beliefs can take up valuable space in your life and steal any chance of peacefulness.

*The simplification of life is one of the steps to inner peace. A persistent simplification will create an inner and outer well-being that places harmony in one's life.*

Peace Pilgrim

## Advantages of inner peace

How do you know if you have inner peace? Some people say it's a powerful feeling that they have deep within, but they can't really explain it to others. Each person has his own unique way of describing it. My pastor, Tom, presented a lesson on inner peace, and this is what he said about it: "Inner peace is a feeling, state of mind, calmness within, and an inner acceptance of self." He said it doesn't mean you are content about everything in your life, but you can accept the place where you are without questioning things. You go through life knowing you will make it just fine. You accept yourself just as you are—faults and all—and it's okay. Did he say that your life doesn't have to be perfect before you can experience inner peace? Yes!

When is the last time you did something good for you? Do you leave yourself out of the equation too many times by doing only for others? True, it gives you a deep peaceful feeling to help others, but at the same time you need to appreciate yourself. One way to experience inner peace is to recharge your battery. We need a warning feature like cameras have, that flashes "weak battery" before it goes completely dead. Wouldn't it be great if you had an internal warning system to tell you it was time to recharge? Feeling drained from constantly doing for others while dealing with your own issues can suck the energy out of you. Life is no longer rewarding and vibrant. How can you get that enthusiasm back? Include only the people, experiences, and needs that add to your life.

Regular self-care revitalizes your energy and your drive. How much time do you spend on thinking about what renews you, what calms you, what makes you feel good on the inside? Do you make time to do the things that bring out the best in you? It's important to value yourself by taking care of your mind, your body, and your soul. Take time to do the things you enjoy, whether it's some form of exercise, a hobby, or just being out in nature. Appreciate yourself by taking time to get a massage, buy those tickets to the play you've wanted to see, pack a lunch and head to the beach, or go visit your long-lost friend that you haven't seen for years. The simple pleasures in life create that "feel good on the inside" feeling.

Inner satisfaction can come from dividing your time between yourself and serving others. Whenever you do for others (friend or stranger), it does much more for you than it does for them. If you have ever done volunteer work, you know how gratifying it makes you feel on the inside. Even the smallest gesture or task you do for someone without being asked is rewarding. The simple things that most of us take for granted seem to mean the most to us. Think of how good it feels when you smile at someone and they smile back, or when someone smiles at you. A simple pat on the back from a friend or your boss to show appreciation can mean more than words. It's the little things that others do for us that we appreciate and remember.

## God's peace

Is your life filled with activities that you want or do things creep in that steal your inner satisfaction and calmness? One of the many titles of the greatest person who ever lived is Prince of Peace. Jesus tells us that inner peace is a benefit we achieve when we live by the spirit. "But the fruit of the Spirit is love, joy, peace, forbearance, kindness, goodness, faithfulness, gentleness and self-control."[2] Living a spiritual life brings inner peace, plus all those other qualities that enhance our everyday lives. *The best way to experience inner peace is to be comfortable with being yourself.*

God provides us with what we need to make it in life, but sometimes we give in to our circumstances and feel overwhelmed and helpless. What happens then to your inner peace and security? These anxieties, worries, doubts, and fears gradually overshadow your clarity and calmness. These consuming feelings hide your true nature and your basic sense of peace. Paul said it best in Philippians 3:13–14: ". . . Forgetting what is behind and straining toward what is ahead, I press on toward the goal to win the prize for which God has called me heavenward in Christ Jesus."

If you can learn to live in the present and forget about what could or should have been, you will be a much happier person. Stop worrying, believe that someone watches over you, and believe in yourself.

*We do not believe in ourselves until someone reveals that deep inside us something is valuable, worth listening to, worthy of our trust, sacred to our touch. Once we believe in ourselves we can risk curiosity, wonder, spontaneous delight or any experience that reveals the human spirit.*

E. E. Cummings

## Explore your creativity

People are happiest when they are doing what they enjoy. When you pursue your dreams and goals, your energy level and creative juices start to overflow. Some of us are confused about what it means to be creative. How do you know if you are creative and how do you develop creativity?

Everyone has a different view of what it means to be creative. For some of us, being creative means creating something from nothing, such as an artist who paints a picture or a songwriter who writes a song. You are creative if you plant a seed and watch it grow into a plant. Solving a problem is being creative.

People like to explain themselves by telling you which side of their brain they use the most. You'll hear statements like, "I'm left brained because I think logically," or, "I'm right brained because I am creative in my thinking." It's best to practice using both sides of your brain. If you only think logically and can't tap into your feelings or your intuition, it is difficult to think creatively. Everyone has a creative side, but you may have to work at bringing out your creativity. It takes a vivid imagination, originality, and a sense of adventure to spark your desire to be different and to create new opportunities and challenges.

Creativity allows you to explore new opportunities. It promotes a spirit within you that sparks excitement and adventure. You feel good about attempting new things or trying different ways to approach a problem or situation. Creativity enhances our imagination by allowing us to ask more questions and to brainstorm new ideas. It opens us up to other peoples' opinions and suggestions, and we are willing to change our own perceptions because of fresh information. The new opportunities that come along will crank up your motivation. The results will gratify you, and you'll wonder why you never tried this before. As your life becomes simpler, you feel happier and healthier about yourself and your environment.

When I point out how creative a certain client is because of how he handled a situation or problem, he often has a confused look and says, "I don't have a creative bone in my body!" He didn't realize that solving a problem is being creative. You don't have to be an artist or musician to have creative talent. Redecorating a room, designing a flowerbed, even making airplanes out of paper is being creative. Creativity is the ability to use your imagination. Imagination allows you to be different, to look at things differently. Being different means you persevere even when others consider you "outside the norm." When you do this, you are creative. You're original. You are yourself.

*Nothing is beyond our reach, for nothing is beyond our imagination, and imagination is the starting point for all progress.*

Jim Rohn

## Roadmap to success

Imagine yourself vacationing on an island with your loved one. You are sitting at a table for two watching the sunset; the waiter pours your favorite wine to go along with your hors d'oeuvres as soft music plays in the background. You're thinking to yourself, what a life! About that time the alarm clock goes off and you awaken to reality. As you shower, you think about how nice it would be if you could live the life you just dreamed of. Wouldn't it be nice if you had a roadmap to lead you to your dreams? You just punch in your destination, and a map appears and tells you how to get there. You wouldn't need to worry about taking the wrong roads or which way to turn. You would just follow the directions.

Some people describe living their lives as simply staying between the white lines on the road as they travel. They have no set destination; they just follow the lines and go wherever the lines go. With no goal in mind, these people have no idea where they will end up. People who live like this remind me of that saying I once read: "Expect nothing and you won't be disappointed."

But there are others who prefer to decide which road they will take. They know what they want out of life. As you live your life, what gives your life meaning? Is it your work, your family, your friends? Do your life circumstances empower you to exceed your possibilities? Are your strengths, abilities, and knowledge creating enjoyable opportunities for you? If so, you are living a powerful and fulfilling life in which you are the driver.

Most of us, whether we realize it or not, do have a map for our lives. It appears when we use our exceptional talents and abilities. Problems come along when we don't believe we have special talents. Do not minimize your strengths—your special,

God-given inner power—that provides you with the necessary tools to obtain any goal that you choose to pursue. Use them! Start now to explore the things that bring you peace, joy, freedom, happiness, and success. These in turn will guide you in creating your unique roadmap to life.

*And in the end, it's not the years in your life that count. It's the life in your years.*

Abraham Lincoln

## It's your life!

Your life is your story. It is being written daily, chapter by chapter, as you live it. Are you the author of your story? There is controversy around this question. If you are a Christian and spiritual, God is the creator and author of your life. He created us in His image, but He gives us the freedom to live our lives as we choose. He wants us to live life to the fullest and allow Him to be our guide. He lets us hold the pen and do the actual writing as He watches over us.

On the other hand, if you aren't spiritual, you would say you are the author of your life. In either case, you should be the one actually writing your story. What I mean is, don't let others write your story for you. When you allow others to dictate how you should live your life, then they are the author. Maybe you'll be making suggestions, but you are still allowing someone else to take charge. If you are not the author, you may want to take over now, because you only have one life to live. Don't waste another minute!

The content that fills the pages of your story is constantly being written by you as you live it. The characters, the main points, the plot, the things you want to change or edit, and the empowering material that fills your life will be decided by you. You can choose who you want and don't want in your story. As you face your life situations, some pleasant and others challenging, the lessons you learn along the way will either strengthen you or tear you down. The story's ending will also be decided by you.

How do you know if you are on the right path? How do you feel about your life right now? Are you stressed, frustrated, have no specific direction or focus, or do you feel content, satisfied, and happy about the way your life is going? By answering these questions honestly, you will know if you are going down the right path. If you are committed to taking the steps necessary to reach your goals and make the desired changes, you will feel a sense of inner peace and outward satisfaction. These will be borne out in your attitude, behavior, and the results of your changes. You achieve, and others around you will notice. You seek and find a greater meaning in life because you are the author of your life, not merely a character.

When you feel stuck and you can't move forward for some reason, your path may need to be changed. Maybe it's time to reconsider your goals. Are your goals right for you? If you spend more time trying to get out of doing a task instead of being passionate about it, that's a warning sign that something is not right. Ask yourself what's holding you back? You might be struggling because you are doing what others think you should do instead of following your heart. If so, it's time for you to change your direction and decide which route is best for you.

*The best day of your life is the one on which you decide your life is your own. No apologies or excuses. No one to lean on, rely on, or blame. The gift is yours—it is an amazing journey—and you alone are responsible for the quality of it. This is the day your life really begins.*

Bob Moawad

Once at a funeral, a minister said that the two things you pay the most attention to on a tombstone are the date of birth and the date of death. Then he said something that got everyone's attention. It's the dash between these dates that is really the most important, because the dash tells the story of the person who died. Who was this person, how did he live his life, what did he do during his lifetime, what do others say about him, and is the world a better place because he lived in it? Behind the dash is where you find the answers.

When you are actively designing your roadmap, you are filling in the answers to these questions:

- Are you doing the things that are important to you?
- Do you know what makes you feel satisfied and fulfilled?
- Are your daily actions guided by your unique principles and values?
- How do you determine what is right or wrong?
- What are your priorities?

Use your values to decide if you are putting first things first. You don't want to waste time by doing the things that are not truly important. Don't forget to include others. Make time for the people you care about and the ones who care about you. Take the time to have fun with your family and friends. Reconnect with old friends that have played an important part in your life.

Continue to work on your personal, professional, and spiritual development through living your specific purpose. You'll know you are living through your purpose when, as you reach your goals, you have a sense of satisfaction and fulfillment that comes from deep within and that shows on the outside. It is meaningful for you to share your life blessings with others. You are driven to be yourself, no pretense, because you are comfortable with yourself. The strong sense of inner satisfaction will continue to guide you toward your goals and help you discern what and who to allow into your life.

## God's roadmap

God created the major roadmap. We have the pen, but He has the ink. He realized we would need driving directions as we design our unique roadmap. As you travel on your journey, you will face sharp curves, detours, and closed roads. You can be reassured that He will not lead you in the wrong direction, because we are told to trust in the Lord with all our heart and not to trust our own understanding (Prov. 3:5–6). If you acknowledge and serve God wholeheartedly, He will make your path less complicated. He will lead you to a more abundant and peaceful journey than you could ever imagine.

## Creating life's map—your journey begins

Together let's design your special roadmap so you can have the kind of life you deserve. Take these Action Steps and hold yourself accountable to do them. As you create your unique plan, critique your progress often by using these four *R*s:

- **R**emember—where you are.
- **R**eminder—where you want to be.
- **R**enewal—take the steps to stay committed to your life mission.
- **R**ejoice—celebrate your accomplishments and reap the benefits of your new life.

## Call to Action Steps:

❖ Start a new habit of thinking positive. Pay special attention to your language. If you often use negative phrases, such as "I can't," "It won't work," or "I'm not," you are probably a negative thinker.

Example:

1. Using negative statements limits your potential and takes away your initiative. Be more aware of how often you use negative phrases. Before you reply to someone, stop and think about your answer.

2. Change your thought processes to the positive. Think to yourself and answer "I'll try" or "It might work," instead of immediately giving a negative answer. Do this often, and gradually your thinking will change from negative to positive.

3. Ask some of your friends to remind you when you start talking or acting negatively so you can immediately stop it.

4. Hang around positive people, as they are much happier and more focused.

5. Look up positive affirmations. Find some that you like and place them where you can read them often. Live by these affirmations and before you know it, you'll be able to overcome the hurdles in life and see your challenges as stepping stones to a better you. Add new affirmations often.

❖ Think of ways you can simplify your life. Think of your reasons why you want to have a simpler life.

Example:

1. Spend more time with your family, have less stress, or more time for you.

2. Keep your goals in the forefront of your mind. Make a list of all your commitments at work and in your personal life. Include hobbies, clubs, online groups, civic groups, your kids' activities, sports, household chores, etc.

3. Select the activities that give you satisfaction, enjoyment, or benefit you in some way. If possible, toss the rest. It might be difficult to do it at first, but you can limit your commitments.

4. Cut back on the things that you really don't need in your life. You might need to de-clutter your home or cut back on the amount of time you spend watching TV or using your electronic devices.

5. The bottom line is to create a life that only includes the commitments you enjoy and want to do. Save some quiet time for you. Watch you don't fill up your life again once you simplify it.

❖ Once you have simplified your life, search within you to see what gives you inner peace. Take the time to do something that rewards you with a calm, relaxing, and peaceful feeling. Write down things you would like to try that would bring out those feelings.

Examples:

1. Have a massage, attend a yoga class, sit on the beach and watch the waves, witness a sunrise or sunset, take a walk through the woods.

2. If you are spiritual, find a quiet place to read the Bible—maybe with your morning coffee—or attend a Bible study.

3. Do things to improve your health, including proper nutrition and adequate sleep and exercise. Try to plan minivacations instead of waiting for your main summer vacation. Make special time for you to dwell on your future goals and plans. Pick the things that are unique to you.

❖ Do things to bring out your creativity. Think of activities you would like to try but haven't because you are afraid you'll look silly. Take chances and don't worry what others will think.

Example:

1. You have this gnawing feeling deep within that you want to write a book, even though you know nothing about writing. You push the feeling aside but the thought keeps resurfacing. One day you say something to a friend about a subject you are passionate about, and he says, "Wow, you know so much about that, maybe you should write a book!" There's your proof that it's more than just a feeling. You are meant to take action and write your book. You may need to do a lot of research to find out how to begin, but you'll be so excited, it won't be difficult.

2. Another way to develop your creativity is to see things differently. If you have a problem you are trying to solve, think outside the box. Write down every solution you can think of, even the silly ones. Sometimes the best answers come from being relaxed and funny. Look at cartoons, since they often make light of tough situations. Being creative can come from a simple idea that you turn into your project. Take initiative, use your imagination, and your simple idea may become your next job.

❖ Draft your life plan. After you write down your plan, put a specific date on it so you will have a timeline.

Example:

1. Write down the opportunities or jobs you are interested in. Explore and investigate what is available, and then review the requirements and make sure you update your profile to meet those requirements. Give each major event a date for getting it accomplished. Follow through! Be consistent, take small steps, and always reward

yourself each time you make progress. Evaluate your progress often to see if you are still on the right track.

Review this sample drawing of a Life Strategy Plan. If one strategy (plan) is not working, modify it or come up with another one. As you add new strategies, evaluate your plan often to see what works and what doesn't. Keep it simple. Don't overload yourself. Share your plan with others. Be accountable.

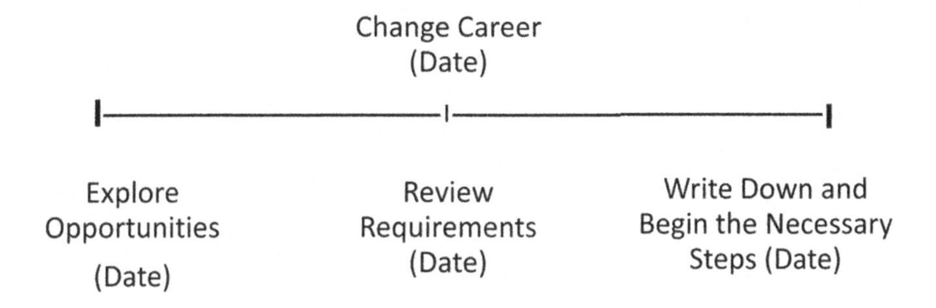


If you are not making progress or feel you are not motivated in reaching a certain goal, it's probably time to update or change your roadmap. You can choose to change the plans to accommodate your style or come up with a new outline entirely to achieve your goals. If you actually write out a projected plan for your future, it is more likely to happen. You can study it and use it as your motivation to take the necessary steps to reach your goals. By having a strategy that you can occasionally revisit and change, you are more likely to live the life you prefer.

CONCLUSION

# Take Your Show on the Road

*Share your gifts to make a difference. Continue to transform yourself and live a most fulfilled and blessed life.*

**Bless those who challenge us to grow, to stretch, to move beyond the knowable, to come back home to our elemental and essential nature. Bless those who challenge us for they remind us of doors we have closed and doors we have yet to open.**

Navajo saying

## A tribute to you

Congratulations! You took the time and energy to read this book and to focus on your life as it is now. Were you able to identify what's missing from your life right now? More importantly, are you driven and inspired to make the changes that can guide you to living a life more suitable and fulfilling for you?

Please continue to study the material in each chapter that speaks to you. Envision how it will feel when you are comfortable being in charge of your life. *Remember, it's your life. Own it!* When doubt or that gut feeling hangs around, know that there is a reason for it. Ask yourself often, "Is this activity or person I'm tolerating cluttering my life, draining my energy, or motivating me to be the best I can be?" You decide who and what you keep and what to let go of in your life.

Hopefully your life will be more rewarding and you will feel proud of yourself. How you see yourself affects how you see the world around you. When you become empowered, it will be easy for you to share the new you with others. Family, friends, and coworkers will notice the new you and wonder how they can live a more fulfilling life too. The desire to help others will overflow within you, and the differences you make in other people's lives will be gratifying and rewarding.

*Within you right now is the power to do things you never dreamed possible. This power becomes available to you just as soon as you can change your beliefs.*

Maxwell Maltz

Begin today developing a strong positive belief system that will protect you against the inner fears that can creep into your thoughts as you face your daily decisions. You'll notice a stronger discipline to distance yourself from negative people and negative situations. Your self-confidence will improve. Your decision making combined with your positive self-belief will make you more determined to live a life of your choosing. You will be confident about the decisions you make and will face the consequences of those decisions without fear. Instead of stressing over your situation, you'll say, "Bring it on!"

*Expect more of yourself as you discover your unique life purpose and mission.* Set your sights and goals on what you are passionate about and you'll constantly discover strengths from within. Your new ambition will surface and take you to places you never imagined! Take time to reflect on your life often, stay in touch with where you are on your life mission, and continue to build on your personal foundation. Don't build a foundation on sand, which will cave in under the least amount of pressure. Have a firm and solid foundation so that when you need to overcome obstacles, you'll know where you stand. Remember to trust your instincts and be sensitive to your gut feelings. If you are struggling with a decision or difficult situation, it could be time to reassess your value system. You must keep your response to a problem in line with your values and morals.

Your personal growth and self-improvement are invaluable to your happiness. Know that your personal value is not represented by what you own or your job status. You will experience greater personal growth through consistently engaging in activities that enrich your life and by associating with people who inspire you. If something or someone hinders your life mission, quickly decide if you need that situation or person in your life. You know what feels right and what feels wrong. Set boundaries that are in line with your integrity.

*The greatest good you can do for another is not just share your riches, but to reveal to him his own.*

Benjamin Disraeli

Take time often to meditate on your present journey. It's important to allow yourself quiet time to reflect on your emotions and your environment. Do you have inner peace? You will know if you do, because you will feel an inner balance and harmony that manifests itself on the outside through your compassion, love, care, thoughts, and actions. You will be more forgiving toward yourself and others. Because of this, you will become more content, peaceful, relaxed, and confident and will view your life—past, present, and future—differently. It's good to learn from your past mistakes, but don't constantly dwell on them and let them stop you from taking charge of your life.

Try to stay connected with God to gain a new perspective on life. You are not alone on your journey, because God is there to inspire, comfort, and guide you on a path filled with blessings and opportunities created just for you. God is the crafter of our stories. He has given us everything we need to live a fruitful life.

In Hebrews 12:2, we are encouraged to keep our eyes fixed on Jesus as we run our race in life. Jesus endured more than you and I will ever have to endure. He was scorned, shamed, and humiliated in public. He willfully died on the cross because of His love for all of us. Jesus had a strong foundation made of faith, love, and peace. His life philosophy was, and is, to keep the faith no matter what you face. His life mission was to love everyone and to save souls. Jesus's life is our example and inspiration to run our race in faith and to live with others in holiness and peace. He can be your biggest encourager and motivator. Know that the difficult things you endure will increase your faith, and your rewards will far outweigh your present troubles.

Do a frequent analysis of your life. Where do you get your inspiration? How strong is your faith? Has a tragedy stolen your faith? Maybe it's time to get back to your values and to God. Being connected to God can be as simple as talking with Him through prayer. Pray for faith to revive you and to provide you with the strength to remove the walls that are stopping you from being *who* you can be. Be quiet and listen to His answers. God will often bless you by purposely placing certain people in your life. God doesn't want your life to be uneventful, because He knows you can become a better person by dealing with the messiness of life. His desires may not be what you desire. But be thankful for the interruptions in life, the problems that ruin your plans or mess up the way you spend your time. These unnecessary things may be what are needed for you to proceed in life with courage, hope, and inner peace. They may direct you to a better path.

You have what you need. Begin now to live your life with a powerful thirst for courage and trust in your talents and strengths. Look forward to the future with confidence and faith that God will continue to fill you with the living water. Every day we live and breathe is a gift, a gift to live life to the fullest. With your newfound inner peace, you will want to do for others as often as you can. It will be a blessing for you to share your gifts with others. The song "Let There Be Peace on Earth" illustrates what peace can feel like. The words are simple thoughts of peace on earth and how peace can begin with us. Peace does come from within and it can begin with you.

*Appreciate and love yourself!* Know that you will face difficult situations, but you are now better equipped to tackle them. God gave you your own special talents and gifts. No one else has what you have, and He expects you to use them to benefit you, others you come in contact with, and to glorify Him. Again, use the material in this book that reaches out to you and keep it foremost in your mind. It takes practice to change long-developed habits and behavior patterns. No matter what stage you are at in life, you deserve to be happy and peaceful. It's never too late to begin living your life the way you prefer. The past is the past, but the future belongs to you.

*Accept responsibility for your thoughts, actions, and behaviors.* Change what you need to change and keep what is beneficial to you. Each step you take brings you closer to your new transformation. Share with others what you become and what you learn. The goal of this book is not for you to be perfect but to be content with who you are and with the life you create. You, like all of us, are a work in progress.

I leave you with one last action step to do that can assist you in achieving the success you desire. Write your obituary according to how you live your life and the path you are on right now. Evaluate which direction your path is headed and whether it is leading you to where you want to go. After you write your obituary, read it. Now, write a second obituary that includes the things you most want to accomplish, projects you enjoy doing for yourself and for others, and the people you love sharing your life with. This second one will be the one that gives you the desire to make a difference in the lives of others and will inspire you to love your life and make contributions to this world. After doing this activity, you'll have a more positive outlook, will achieve more, and will pay more attention to your everyday choices. Life will be more fulfilling!

Lastly, what I wish for you is to have inner peace and contentment with every aspect of your life. I pray for God's presence and blessings to enter your life in ways that will surpass your wildest dreams. Know that God is all powerful and in charge if you allow Him to be. Isaiah tells us that "those who hope in the Lord will renew their strength. They will soar on wings like eagles; they will run and not grow weary, they will walk and not be faint."[1] Begin your new journey and be ready for a lifelong transformation that will take you to heights you never imagined!

I leave you with this poem by Jacqueline Schiff.

## Don't Ever Forget How Special You Are

Don't ever forget that you are unique. Be your best self and not an imitation of someone else.

Find your strengths and use them in a positive way. Don't listen to those who ridicule the choices you make.

Travel the road that you have chosen and don't look back with regret. You have to take chances to make your dreams happen.

Remember that there is plenty of time to travel another road—and still another—in your journey through life. Take the time to find the route that is right for you.

You will learn something valuable from every trip you take, so don't be afraid to make mistakes.

Tell yourself that you're okay just the way you are. Make friends who respect your true self.

Take the time to be alone, too, so you can know just how terrific your own company can be. Remember that being alone doesn't always mean being lonely; it can be a beautiful experience of finding your creativity, your heartfelt feelings, and the calm and quiet peace deep inside you.

And please don't ever forget that you are special.

# Author Bio

Debbie Miles has worked as a registered nurse for more than twenty years. She is now a licensed clinical social worker in private practice and a life coach. Debbie is president of The Sky Is The Limit Coaching. She is coauthor of the Gratitude Book Project: *Celebrating Moms & Motherhood* and *A Celebration of Personal Heroes*. Debbie lives with her husband in Pensacola Beach, Florida.

# Endnotes

## Introduction

1. www.holybible.com/resources/poems/ps.php?sid=1120.

## Principle 1

1. Luke 6:46–49 (NIV).
2. www.great-quotes.com/quotes/movie/Forrest+Gump.
3. www.bizography.org/biographies/dave-pelzer.html.
4. W. Timothy Gallwey, Edd Hanzelik, and John Horton, *The Inner Game of Stress* (New York: Random House Publishing Company, 2009), 97.
5. www.disabled-world.com/artman/publish/famous-blind.shtml#ixzz18Cx8xB4w.
6. www.cybernation.com/lincoln/persistence.php.
7. Isaiah 40:29, 31 (NIV).

## Principle 2


1. Dave Pelzer, *Help Yourself: Finding Hope, Courage, and Happiness* (New York: Penguin, 2000).

2. www.Spiritual-Short-Stories.com.

3. *The American Heritage Medical Dictionary,* Fifth Edition, s.v. "fear."

4. Glen Hopkins, owner of Motivational-Messages.com.

5. Marianne Williamson, *A Return To Love: Reflections on the Principles of "A Course in Miracles"* (New York: Harper Collins, 1992).

6. Matthew 7:7 (NIV).


## Principle 3


1. www.notablebiographies.com.

2. Margaret Renkl, "Step Outside Your Life," *Ladies Home Journal Vol. CXXVI, Issue No. 1* (January, 2009): 19–22.

3. Matthew 7:8–9 (NIV).

4. Germaine Porché and Jed Niederer, *Coach Anyone About Anything: How to Help People Succeed in Business and Life* (Del Mar, California: Wharton Publishing, Inc., 2001).

5. Matthew 25:14–30 (NIV).

6. Matthew 17:20 (NIV).

7. Deuteronomy 31:6 (NIV).

## Principle 4

1. www.theartofeverydaywonder.com.

2. Ephesians 4:1 (NIV).

3. Bruce Bugbee, *What You Do Best in the Body of Christ: Discover Your Spiritual Gift, Personal Style, and God-Given Passion* (Grand Rapids, Michigan: Zondervan, 2005).

4. Jones, Laurie Beth. *Jesus Life Coach*. New York, New York: MJF Books, Fine Communications, 2004.

5. www.spiritual-short-stories.com.

6. Stephen Covey, *7 Habits of Highly Effective People* (New York: Free Press, 2004).

## Principle 5

1. www.word4life.com/brokenpot.html.

2. Dave Meyer, *The Sage and Scholar's Guide, Coaching Assessments* (Boulder, Colorado: LearnMore Communications, Inc., 2006).

## Principle 6

1. www.hawaiiswim.org/business/TheButterfly/TheButterly

2. Galatians 5:22–23 (NIV).

## Conclusion

1. Isaiah 40:31(NIV).

# Resource and Book Recommendation List

Books are a great resource. This is a partial list of books that I have read and recommend for those who desire to improve their inner and outer strengths. If you have books that you recommend, I would appreciate knowing about them. Enjoy!

## Motivational

*Masters of Success: Proven Techniques for Achieving Success in Business and Life* by Ivan Misner, PhD, and Don Morgan, MA

The authors of this book feel the best route to success is to read real-life stories of others who are becoming successful or have achieved success. It is inspiring to read about how others were motivated to become who and what they are. After reading this book, you will feel more passionate and energetic in reaching your goals.

*The Five Major Pieces to the Life Puzzle* by Jim Rohn

Jim Rohn has been a motivational speaker and personal development trainer for many years. His books are very inspirational, and his unique, simple style of sharing his talents with others is captivating. He died in December 2009.

*The Slight Edge: Secret to a Successful Life* by Jeff Olson

Jeff shares his ideas that will help us put the information already available to us to use. This book is filled with encouraging stories as well as intriguing and thought-provoking questions. It has exercises that help to move us in the right direction.

*Time Power: A Proven System for Getting More Done in Less Time Than You Ever Thought Possible* by Brian Tracy

This is a great self-help book if you want to become more organized. The author explains practical and usable methods and strategies to improve the quality or our lives in every area. Who couldn't use this?

*Become Who You Were Born to Be: We All Have a Gift . . . Have You Discovered Yours?* by Brian Souza

In this book, Mr. Souza provides a blueprint to help you discover your gifts and how you can use them to grow personally and professionally. He provides examples of various top achievers. It's easy to understand.

## Career/Job Decisions

*The 4-Hour Workweek: Escape 9-5, Live Anywhere, and Join the New Rich* by Timothy Ferriss

This book informs us that there is more to life than working all the time. Mr. Ferriss gives a different blueprint for living your life on your own terms. This book is full of valuable resources that are readily accessible.

*48 Days to the Work You Love: Preparing for the New Normal* by Dan Miller

The material in this book assists you in discovering your life purpose within your work. It helps you to implement a plan that allows you to grow spiritually, emotionally, relationally, and as a person. This book is full of valuable resources also.

*Make Today Count: The Secret of Your Success Is Determined by Your Daily Agenda* by John C. Maxwell

The author of this book believes that the way we live our lives today prepares us for tomorrow. He implies that the secret of success is determined by our daily agenda. It is easy to read and has great content.

## Marketing

*Duct Tape Marketing: The World's Most Practical Small Business Marketing Guide* by John Jantsch

The author shares his knowledge about marketing and teaches others how to put this practical knowledge to work in creating a more effective business. He gives step-by-step demonstrations on how to market with integrity. This book is practical and you can put it to use immediately.

*Raving Fans: A Revolutionary Approach to Customer Service* by Ken Blanchard and Sheldon Bowles

Ken Blanchard has written many books and conducts seminars through Blanchard Training and Development, Inc. This book presents a simple philosophy and provides tips and techniques that can help anyone turn their customers into raving, spending fans. A short book filled with great examples.

*Free Prize Inside: How to Make a Purple Cow* by Seth Godin

This book is a marketing book for individuals, managers, and CEOs. This author feels real marketing begins inside your product, not in the pages of a magazine.

## Personal Growth/Inspirational

*Listen to Your Life: Following Your Unique Path to Extraordinary Success* by Valorie Burton

Valorie is a life coach and speaker and has a daily radio feature called *The Good Life* that airs nationwide. This is a spiritual book in which she asks her readers to consider the current state of their relationships, work, and accomplishments. She gives you tools that will allow you to "hear" what your life is saying to you. You will feel propelled to take action while reading this book.

*What's Really Holding You Back?: Closing the Gap between Where You Are and Where You Want to Be* by Valorie Burton

This author believes that even people who know their purpose in life can find themselves living a life that is not what it could be. She feels there is a gap between where we are to where we want to be. The information in this book will help you identify the force that is holding you back and find the courage to conquer it.

*Just Who Will You Be? Big Question. Little Book. Answer Within* by Maria Shriver

Maria Shriver shares her message about the real meaning of life. She believes it is not what you do in life that matters, but who you are. She leaves us with the thought that it is never too late to become the person you want to be.

*Help Yourself: Finding Hope, Courage, and Happiness* by Dave Pelzer

Mr. Pelzer experienced heart-wrenching struggles as the person who should have loved him the most abused him. He has turned his struggles into victories, and he shares how to overcome adversity and take charge of your life. He urges you to move past the pain. He provides examples of others who have faced hardships as well.

*The Inner Game of Stress* by W. Timothy Gallwey, Edd Hanzelik, MD, and John Horton, MD

These authors illustrate how stress affects every aspect of our well-being. Mr. Gallwey explains how negative thoughts alter our self-worth. He feels we have the means to guard ourselves against a stressful life. We just need to tap into our inner resources to enjoy a positive and successful life. This book includes worksheets, case histories, and self-help tools.

*Happy for No Reason: 7 Steps to Being Happy from the Inside Out* by Marci Shimoff, with Carol Kline

In this book, Ms. Shimoff presents seven steps to finding happiness from the inside out. She includes several questionnaires, exercises, and personal interviews of others and what happiness means to them. She provides many tools that can be applied instantly to your life.

*Jesus Life Coach: Learn from the Best* by Laurie Beth Jones

Through the material in this book, the author presents practical ways to incorporate Jesus's teachings and practical advice into our life strategies. She provides ways to use this material in your personal and professional life. There are thought-provoking questions at the end of each chapter.

## Assessments/Tests

*The Passion Test: The Effortless Path to Discovering Your Life Purpose* by Janet Bray Attwood and Chris Attwood

These authors show us the importance of focusing on the things that are most important in our lives. The information is thought provoking and will guide you in finding your passion in life. This book contains action steps and a passion test.

*Strengths Finder 2.0* by Tom Rath

This book presents various strategies that help you recognize and apply your strengths. You learn the value and importance of focusing on your strengths, not your weaknesses. Useful action ideas are located at the end of the chapters. There is an access code in the back of the book that allows you to do the Strengths Finder 2.0 Assessment on the Internet.

## Spiritual Gifts/Assessments

*What You Do Best in the Body of Christ: Discover Your Spiritual Gifts, Personal Style, and God-Given Passion* by Bruce Bugbee

This book increases your awareness about spiritual gifts. The author believes God has a purpose for everyone, and that He gave all of us a special gift(s). By using our gifts, our lives will have a greater meaning and impact in the world. There are thought-provoking questions at the end of the chapters. Spiritual gift assessments are provided also.

*Spiritual Gift: Their Purpose and Power* by Bryan Carraway

This author approaches spiritual gifts in an objective manner. He discusses the purpose and power of spiritual gifts. Mr. Carraway addresses how awareness of these gifts will encourage us to fulfill our God-given vocation or calling. A spiritual gifts assessment is included also.

www.churchgrowth.org. Free spiritual gifts assessment for individual and groups.

## Spiritual/Christian

*Crazy Love: Overwhelmed by a Relentless God* by Francis Chan, with Danae Yankoski

Mr. Chan discusses the importance of your unique belief in God. He asks questions and discusses material that causes you to consider how you praise God. This book encourages you to examine yourself as you are on your spiritual journey. This book can be used for individual or group Bible studies.

*Healing the Wounded Heart: Removing Obstacles to Intimacy with God* by Thom Gardner

This book can be used as a personal study to assist in healing emotional scars from the past. The author recommends reading this material for inner healing. I recommend this book for many of my clients who have difficulties moving forward because of wounded emotions. The author provides a simple biblical format and process.

*Deadly Emotions: Understand the Mind-Body-Spirit Connection That Can Heal or Destroy You* by Don Colbert, MD

Dr. Colbert stresses the importance of overcoming the deadly emotions that can trigger a disease process. He discusses how various emotions such as anger, depression, and stress can bring about or worsen diseases. He relates how diseases can affect each area of our life: physical, emotional, and spiritual.

*Tragic Redemption: Healing the Guilt and Shame* by Hiram Johnson

This author knows firsthand, because of his tragic accident, the importance of healing the guilt and shame within. Hiram describes in his autobiography how to reframe the “dark side” of personality in order to claim redemption. He uses biblical scripture and addresses the need for God's love, grace, and power for us to live more peaceful and meaningful lives. This book will touch your heart in a special way.